Modern Fishing
General Editor:

FLY FIS

Spawning trout

FLY FISHING

BY

VISCOUNT GREY OF FALLODON

*WITH WOOD ENGRAVINGS
BY ERIC FITCH DAGLISH*

ANDRE DEUTSCH

First published 1899

Revised, enlarged and illustrated edition 1930

Reprinted 1984 by André Deutsch Limited
105 Great Russell Street London WC1

Introduction copyright © 1984 by Antony Atha

ISBN 0 233 97643 4

Printed in Great Britain by
Ebenezer Baylis & Son Limited
The Trinity Press, Worcester, and London

INTRODUCTION

If ever in some nightmareish Orwellian future a totalitarian state were to limit me to one book on fishing, this is the one that I would choose. *Fly Fishing* was first published in 1899 as part of the Haddon Hall Library and re-issued in 1930 when Lord Grey added two new chapters at the end of the book; *Spring Salmon Fishing—The Cassley*, and *Retrospect*. I have chosen the revised edition for this series.

Why is this book such a classic? Why, among so many fishing books written by so many fishing authorities, should this be the one book that is read over and over again by so many fishermen. Grey was a thoughtful, skilful angler with considerable powers of perseverence and observation, but he was no great innovator. He did not invent greased line fishing for salmon or nymph fishing for chalk-stream trout. He did not, as far as we can tell, dress his own flies nor is any famous fly named after him. The reason why this book strikes such a chord of response is that no writer has ever been better at putting into words those emotions and feelings that are experienced by every fisherman.

One of the very few fishing triumphs of my life took place many years ago on Loch Skeen. A cousin and I walked up there after lunch one Sunday, really to see how quickly we could climb the Grey Mare's Tail. When we got to the water there, we found a number of other fishermen and a mass of small trout rising with a constant determination all over the loch. They would look at none of the standard loch flies and I and the other anglers caught nothing. Then I noticed some small dark flies blowing onto the water from the heather round the banks, and I found that the trout would accept a small, dark Greenwell's Glory, fished dry, as a substitute. My fishing diary tells me I caught 27. As we returned home passing the other anglers I had to reveal my basket and fly in response to the inevitable question. 'Dry fly,' said a Border worthy, shaking his head, 'A' doon't know aboot thaat.' and I felt like Lord Grey after his day on the Dart when his inquisitor told him 'Dry fly. We know nothing about dry fly here.' I am sure that both our questioners 'went on their ways with thoughts that were not very kind'.

And so every fisherman should read this book. Not because it will enable him to catch more fish; not because it provides any original insights into fishing techniques; but because of the description of days spent by the river; for the recollection of the emotions of all anglers; for the variety of fishing that is described. For this is an all-round fishing book. I know no better description of burn fishing with a worm, what fun it was; no better description of boyhood triumphs; nor of the emotions of the fisherman who has searched out some distant voe in the Shetlands and spent a fruitless wet morning casting in vain round the seaweed, seeing nothing, catching nothing, feeling nothing, the immense hopelessness and pointlessness of the exercise growing in his mind with every cast.

One thing must be added. The book ends sadly. There is a grandeur and majesty about this recollection but it is one of mourning for something that had passed. Grey was Foreign Secretary at the outbreak of the First World War and felt the horror of that holocaust in a very personal way. He also went blind. *Retrospect*, the last chapter of the book, reflects these feelings. Yet the last two pages are the most beautiful apologia for a fisherman's life ever written. They should be printed separately, framed, and given to every angler.

Antony Atha

PUBLISHER'S NOTE

WHEN Lord Grey agreed to a new edition of his book with wood engravings by Eric Fitch Daglish, he said that he would like to re-read the work and to make any small corrections which might be necessary. He had no wish to alter the shape or substance of the book, which has enjoyed some thirty years' popularity. But in re-reading it he found that he had perhaps something more to say. The two new chapters, "Spring Salmon Fishing—the Cassley" and "Retrospect," are the result. They take up their natural position at the end of the work, the original form of which is unchanged, except that the Editor's general preface to the Haddon Hall Library, in which *Fly Fishing* first appeared, is omitted, and the original illustrations are replaced by the new wood engravings.

July 1930.

CONTENTS

LIST OF FULL PAGE ILLUSTRATIONS

CHAPTER I

INTRODUCTORY

It would be delightful to write about pleasures, if by doing so one could impart them to others. Many of us, if we had this gift, would no doubt take the world by storm to-morrow, with an account of the delights of living in the country.

Unfortunately, nothing is more difficult than to convey any strong impression of pleasure which has been felt within us, and probably it is only some unconscious egotism which ever prompts us to suppose that it might be easy. The insuperable difficulty lies in the nature of people and things. We do not all care for the same pleasures, and do not want to hear about those of other people. There are even men and women who do not care to play golf, and prefer to avoid the subject ; and all of us, in talking about a hobby, run the risk that our words may fall upon unwilling ears. Sympathy will not flow unless interest is felt, and this latter is a slow growth. The interest that springs up on the spur of the moment is not intelligent ; to be satisfactory either to listener or speaker, it must have a firm root in remembered feelings and associations. Nor must it be taken for granted that an interest felt by people in the same subject necessarily implies a common pleasure. One man may care for

flowers because he likes to live amongst them and loves
the effects of landscape gardening : another because he
studies the life and growth of a plant, and takes infinite
pains to bring individual plants to perfection and to
produce a perfect bloom : a third may care less to grow
the flower than to examine it scientifically ; and so the
pleasure may vary through all degrees, from the highest
and driest botany to the most unlearned sensuous
appreciation of colour, scent, and form.

As a rule, we find our pleasures in our own way for
ourselves, and do not take or learn them from others.
What we really care for we have at first hand, the
beginning of the feeling being within us or not at all,
though what we read or hear from others helps and
stimulates it. It is indeed almost impossible to justify
a particular pursuit to some one else who has not got
the sense of it. One man has a hobby and may talk
about it to another easily, or even with eloquence and
power ; but if that other has not shared the hobby, he
will not understand the language, and the speaker has
no right to expect that he should. On the other hand,
to any one who does share it, even a little imperfectly
told becomes interesting, and weak words begin to stir
kindred memories. When a man has a hobby it is to
be hoped that he will learn reticence ; that he will never
go into the world at large without a resolve not to talk
about what he cares for most ; that in society and places
where they talk, he will carry his delight within him
like a well guarded treasure, not to be unlocked and
disclosed in all its fullness on any slight or trivial
inquiry. Rather let him not use his own key for him-

self, being sure that the test of any really kindred spirit will be the possession of a master key which will open this special door of his mind for him. It is seldom enough that this happens. Most of us live wherever circumstances decide that we should, and live the life that our work requires. We think of our pleasures in night watches, in passing from one place to another, upon the pavement, in trains and cabs ; but the prospect on any given occasion of meeting such a really kindred spirit seems almost too good to be true. If, then, a book is written about a pursuit like fishing, it should be not to preach, or to convert, or to dogmatize. Books about sport and country life should be written and read, partly perhaps for the sake of hints, information, and instruction, but much more in the hope that the sense of refreshing pleasure, which has been felt by the writer, may slide into a sympathetic mind.

There remains yet another difficulty, that of expressing pleasure at all. It may be that language lends itself more easily to forms of argument and thought than of feeling. An argument is something which can be caught and held down and strapped into sentences, but after reading an account of a day's fishing, it is continually borne in upon one that, when all has been said, the half has not been told ; it is not because there is really nothing to tell, as some cynical and unsympathetic mind may suppose ; rather, I think it is because of the nature of joy. Feelings of delight come unsought and without effort—when they are present they are everywhere about and in us like an atmosphere ; when they are past it is almost as

impossible to give an account of them as it is of
"last year's clouds," and the attempt to analyse and
reconstruct the sense of joy that has been and may be
again, seems to result in rows of dead words.

It is worth while to consider some of the different
ways in which authors of repute have written about
angling. Walton, of course, stands first ; his book has
become a classic, and has been read and remembered
now long enough for us to be sure that it will remain
so. This, no doubt, is due to his literary skill, and
to that distinguished something called style, which
Walton had, and without which no book lives long.
There is no definition of style which is satisfactory, or
which tells how it may be acquired, for when a man
has it, what he has is his own and no other's : without
him that particular style would never have been, and
no one else can produce the same effect by imitating it.
It must therefore in some way be the result of the
man's personality ; and the charm of Walton's *Complete
Angler* is at any rate partly due to the simplicity and
purity of nature, which find expression in his book.
There is a quiet and benign light in his writing, which
draws us to it, and makes us choose to linger over it.
It must not, however, be forgotten that Walton wrote
other books not about angling : these, too, are of
literary excellence, and we still have to account for the
fact, that it is by the *Complete Angler* that Walton is
best remembered. It may be that the others would
not have been forgotten ; but unless he had written the
Complete Angler, Walton would never have been as
well known as he is. It is his best book, and I like

to think that it is so, because the happiness of the subject was specially suited to his kind and quiet spirit. Walton took a wide view of the pleasures of angling ; he was of too sensitive a nature to neglect what was to be seen and heard around him, and the object of Piscator is at least as much to teach his scholar to enjoy the spirit of places, times, and seasons, as to catch fish. None the less is Walton careful of instructions in the art of angling. In imparting these he had at any rate the advantage of believing that what he had to teach was new, and he enters into details of baits and tackles and methods, with a zest and confident interest which are hardly possible now. There is an impression of freshness and leisure which never leaves us as we read Walton. The delight of days spent by the river is described as if he felt himself to be the teller of good tidings, in which whosoever wished might share. There is a detachment of mind about him, a sense of freedom and length of days, to which it is less easy to attain in these times of trains, letters, telegrams, and incessant news. There were years in Walton's life of civil war, of great disturbance, public misfortune, and excitement, but it was nevertheless more possible in that age to have long intervals undisturbed and to feel remote. With the exception of Gilbert White's *Selborne,* I know no book in which it is so easy for a tired mind to find refuge and repose as in the *Complete Angler.*

As a contrast to Walton it is interesting to consider Charles Kingsley. He, too, has written delightfully about fishing ; there is an onset of enthusiasm in such

a piece as *Chalk Stream Studies* which must stimulate
the keenness of any angler, and Kingsley has a good
store of knowledge of plants, insects, birds, and all the
life about a river. Who would not have kindled at
the thought of a day's fishing with Kingsley ? Who
would not have been the better for it ? but any of us
might have been somewhat exhausted at the end of it.
Kingsley was nobly keen, and he never for one moment
leaves us in doubt of the strength and sincerity of his
affection for all that was interesting and beautiful out
of doors. Every one should know more and fish
better after reading him, but he was a strong mind in
earnest, and he wrote so strenuously that in reading
him I tremble a little, for fear he may strike too hard,
if a big fish should rise. The time, too, in which
Kingsley wrote, was so different from Walton's ; so
much more was known that knowledge seemed to have
a sort of completeness. It is never really so. New
discoveries are being made as frequently as ever, but for
all that, the edges of our knowledge seem now more
clearly defined. Walton has much to tell us ; but
round all his knowledge is a border land of mystery,
of things left uncertain and still to be revealed. His
Fordidge trout belongs to another world than that in
which we move : we feel as if, were we in his place, we
should long to set out upon our travels to find it. It is
not even certain whether a winch should be used, and
if so whether it should be placed upon the butt or the
middle of the rod. Walton feels that all he has to
tell us is visibly leading to some new discovery, which
any man with a good will may hope to make in his

lifetime. In Kingsley's time, and still more now, this delicious sense of impending discovery has gone. Fish and flies are classified and indexed. We may still argue some points, such as the number of different species of *salmonidæ*, or whether fish have a keen perception of colour ; but we know enough to be dogmatic and to make even things which are still uncertain appear not to be open questions. As to rods, tackle, and landing-nets, we are almost weary of the number of inventions, and hardly wish for anything new.

I have taken Walton and Kingsley as two types of appreciative writers about angling : Walton of course, because he is the best of all ; and Kingsley, partly for the sake of contrast in time and temperament, and partly because his vigour as a writer makes it interesting to see how he treats the subject which he loved. Of those who preceded Walton, or were his contemporaries, an interesting and excellent account is to be found in *Walton, and the Earlier Fishing Writers*, by Mr. Marston. Of writers in the earlier part of this century there are names to which many of us are grateful, while in later years one instructive book has followed another, showing more and more tendency to deal separately with each special branch of angling. Many men are good all-round anglers, but these are the days of experts and scientific study, and we write not of all that we know, but of what we know best.

I do not profess to have acquired enough scientific knowledge to enable me to give complete instruction, but even if I could do this there would be no need for me to attempt it now. There are so many splendid manuals of instruction, that any angler, who wishes to get technical knowledge, can learn the very best and latest that is known from more than one recent book about each special branch of angling. It is not therefore my object to teach the art of angling. But if I am ambitious to be an expert at all, it is with regard to the pleasure of angling. I am ready now to yield the palm for skill to whoever chooses to claim it, but I do cherish a belief that I am entitled to rank high among those whose reputation as anglers is measured, not by skill, but by their devotion to angling, and by the delight which they have in it. A chief object of this little book will be to express some of this pleasure, to explain some of its qualities and virtues, and to say how it is that we who are anglers congratulate ourselves upon having one of the best and most wonderful recreations that have ever been known to man.

There may be some natures whose work is pleasure, and who have therefore neither care nor need for any things but work and rest. It is possible to imagine that the pleasure and the work of a poet or an artist may be so interdependent that one cannot exist without giving a direct impulse to the other ; that the feelings for instance of a poet, when heightened by pleasure, lead so continually to efforts to express them, that they themselves seem to be but a motive or preparation for the work of life rather than a thing apart from it. The same may be true of some men of science : there have been men who have seemed to value leisure and energy solely for the sake of observation and research, who have asked for nothing in life except that they should not be interrupted in the pursuit of knowledge. But few people are made entirely like these, and most of us do some work, not from choice, but being either compelled by necessity, or else urged to it by circumstances or some stern inner motive. If work be worthy or noble the greatest satisfaction of life is to be found in doing it well ; the exercise of his highest powers or qualities is the glory of man's being, and the discovery or development of them by use transcends all pleasure. But not all work is of this kind, and in most if not in all of it there is much drudgery, so that we are tormented from time to time by a strong desire to get away from it ; we seem to be doing it, not because we have any genius or gifts for it, but because we are not better suited for anything else. Men whose task is imposed by necessity may well feel that the struggle for something which is not work, for opportunities of recreation, is not only legitimate and just, but imperative. On the other hand, if complete idleness be possible, we are again tormented by the sense of waste or of power unused, by the thought that everything leads to nothing, by the " weight of chance desires " increasing till it produces intolerable restlessness, and the curse of the wandering Jew seems to be working in our nature. Therefore it is that most of us endeavour to divide our lives into three parts, work, rest, and recreation ; and it is with the management of the third part, and the place of angling with regard to it, that this book is concerned.

We probably wish our recreation to be not only apart from our work, but in contrast to it, and those who labour with their brain indoors seek for exercise and open air, use for the body as well as freedom for the mind. Youth asks for something more, and finds it in excitement. These are the three great requisites for the recreation of healthy vigorous boyhood— exercise, open air, and excitement. They are to be found in fine quality in games and in sport, and in both it is probably excitement which at first we care for most consciously. As we grow older a change takes place. Let us analyse, for instance, the pleasure in games. At first we desire only to win—we think only of that; we play the game as boys read an exciting story, with a feverish anxiety to know the end. The next stage, as we grow older, is more intelligent, and we begin to understand the qualities of good play. We improve year by year, and take pride in the increase of our own physical prowess, of which the limit is not yet seen. Then from understanding we pass to an artistic admiration of good play for its own sake; we become judges of how the thing should be done, and we are critics of style. Competition is then desired, not solely for the excitement it provides, but as a stimulus to good play; we no longer seriously expect to improve in our own play, but we take pleasure in doing our best. The last stage may be a long one; it begins with the admission that we are past our best. Strength is not diminished, and indeed we may even have more sheer strength than ever, but the effort of using it has become greater. The first sign of deterioration is when our powers seem as great, but it becomes more exhausting to exert them, and when in a hard

game we do not last so well. The next symptom
follows very soon; we cannot do so quickly what can
no longer be done so easily; our performance suggests
retrospect; the personal element wanes, and we find
satisfaction more and more in contemplation and less
and less in excitement and competition; at last we sit
among the onlookers, and are advised by our friends to
practise golf. There is much that is analogous to all
this in the pleasure which is found in sport.

It would be tedious and perhaps invidious to enter
here upon a comparison of angling with other sports.
Each man sees special advantages in his own favourite
pursuit, and possibly pays for this by overlooking some
advantages which are to be found elsewhere. One
thing I must claim, at any rate for fly fishing, that it
involves less pain than is inflicted in any other sport.
All experience and observation go to prove that what
the fish suffers from most is fright, and this is an
objection which may be brought equally against netting,
and indeed against any possible method of killing fish
except by poison or dynamite, of which the former is
repulsive and horrible, whilst the latter causes wholesale
and ruthless waste of life. Wordsworth calls angling
" the blameless sport," and with his opinion on such
a point any one may be content. Having said so
much, I will for the rest make an appreciation of the
pleasures of angling as little comparative with other
sports as may be.

In angling, as in games, the earliest obvious charac-
teristic is the desire for success and the consequent
excitement. To those who are born-anglers, this

excitement presents a peculiarly attractive and irresistible aspect. There is first the expectation of a bite or a rise, the sudden thrill when it comes, and directly a fish is hooked the overwhelming rush of anxiety as to whether it will be landed. There is more than this ; there is the spirit which seems to enter into the rod and line in playing a fish. They who do not feel these things will never care much for fishing. Probably it is some subtle quality of temperament which makes the difference between men in this respect, but those who are anglers will probably admit that in early boyhood, or at the first opportunity, they felt the excitement of these things, and were captivated by it. For myself I know nothing which equals the excitement of having hooked an unexpectedly large fish on a small rod and fine tackle. One instance, which occurred not so long ago, comes often to mind. I happened one September to be fishing for sea trout, with a single-handed rod, in a long stretch of deep still water, peat coloured, but fairly clear. The day was bright, one of those fine summer days with a light east breeze, enough to make some but only a little ripple. It was necessary, therefore, to use as fine gut as I dared, and small flies, and even then my success was not great. One good sea trout of nearly four pounds was hooked and landed, and several fish were seen, but only occasionally would one rise, and then always very shyly. Late in the afternoon, when the breeze had nearly died away, and hope was getting less, there was a great and sudden boil in the water, one of my flies was seized most unexpectedly, and I knew that either a salmon or grilse was

"One of my flies was seized most unexpectedly"

hooked.   The river at this point was not very wide.
There were two alder bushes growing on the bank, one
above and the other below me, over which no rod could
be passed, but the space in between them must have
been quite two hundred yards of still water, and the
fish being about in the middle of this stretch, there was
no immediate cause for dreading a catastrophe.   But
there were formidable difficulties : one was, that there
was no shallow water to which the fish could be taken ;
another, that the bank was steep and fringed with
rushes ; and a third was, that I had only a trout landing net, not large or strong, and with a weak handle.
There came on me a grim consciousness that the whole
affair must be very long, and that the most difficult
part of all would be at the end, not in playing the fish,
but in landing it.   By slow degrees the fish came under
control of the rod, but the nearer he could be brought
the more were matters complicated by the rushes at
the edge.   Time after time he passed under my eyes,
swimming upright though slowly, so that I could see
shape and size and the marks on the body ; but the end
seemed as far off as ever.   Not till he was at the top
of the water, and it was possible to keep him quiet there,
must anything be risked.   The fish could not be
brought within reach of my hand owing to the rushes.
The bottom of the river was too soft, and the water
too deep at every part for wading.   The small net was
the only chance, and the risk of using it was so great
that I hardly dared to try.   It seemed as if any attempt
to land the fish with this net would precipitate a
catastrophe, which I could not face.   More than once

I failed, and each failure was horrible. The fish was got partly into the net, but moved and splashed out of it, and the nearer each attempt came to success, the greater was the danger. At last, not only the head but enough of the bulk of the body sank into the net. I lifted it; there was a feeling of weakness, a sound of something giving way; the handle bent and the net drooped. I dropped the rod, and somehow with both hands carried or dragged everything up the bank. The salmon weighed eight pounds ten ounces, and it had taken perhaps half an hour to land it. There was no physical reason for being exhausted, and yet for a little time I could do nothing. All power had gone from me ; my limbs were trembling, and there was a looseness of the knees which made it difficult to walk. Such are the great times of sheer excitement which happen in fishing.

It is the plain indiscriminating desire for success which leads us to the second stage in angling, that of taking the pains and trouble necessary to acquire skill. In early years we are content to catch fish anyhow, even with a worm in flooded water. But rivers are for the most part not in flood; on most days in the season, if trout are to be caught at all, it must be in clear water, and we find, too, except in a certain part of the season, that the greatest number can be hooked by using artificial flies. It becomes our object to learn this art and to improve in it by practice. At first the young angler, wholly bent upon success, may value his skill chiefly for its results : he dwells upon these, compares each good day with his own previous records, is probably competitive and anxious that on any given day his basket should be as heavy as those of others who have been fishing the same water. Whenever his basket is heavier than his rival's, he is delighted, and is probably not a little disappointed if, when he thinks he has done well, he finds at the end of the day that some one else has done much better. There is an age at which nearly every one who is keen must be competitive, but as long as this lasts an angler has not yet attained to the greatest enjoyment of his sport. He is missing more pleasure than he gains ; and he is preventing himself from having that detachment of mind, and freedom and independence of spirit, which are among the charms of angling. An angler who is keen will work hard, but he should do it without the sense of strain which comes from trying to beat his own records, or those of others. By all means let us find satisfaction to the end in having a heavy or the heaviest basket, but do not let us make this the prime object of the day. Rather let each day's enjoyment stand upon its own merits without being made comparative.

As our skill increases we reach the third stage, that of caring for skill more for its own sake and less entirely for the results. There comes to be some satisfaction in doing things well, even when the results are not great, in continuing to throw a long line straight and lightly even when fish are rising badly, or in putting a dry fly perfectly to a trout in a difficult place though he refuses to take it. Some measure of success, of course, is always desired, and a man must surely be a pedant, or a prig, to be content to fish all day without it ; but for all that, there is a certain delight in fishing water well, which for a time at any rate is independent of results.   This is especially the case at the beginning of the day, when, for the first hour or so, to know or to think that we are deserving success contents us.

What are the qualities which a man most needs to become a good angler ?   Let us assume that he starts with keenness, that the prospect of hooking a fish produces in him that feeling of excitement which is the motive for a desire to succeed, is the beginning of delight in angling, and, like a first element, cannot be analysed.   What are the other qualities which he must possess or cultivate in order to become really skilful ?   He must, in the first place, have enough strength and aptitude of body to enable him to do a fairly hard day's work and manage both a rod and a fish cleverly, though he will not require the same exceeding quickness of limb, accuracy of eye, and strength, which are necessary to the greatest success in the finest games.   Quickness and delicacy of touch, and a certain power of managing a rod and line, akin to that individual cleverness or genius which men show in the use of tools or instruments with which they are experts, are necessary to success in angling.   The art of throwing a fly well cannot be taught by description ; it may be seen and watched, but it can only be acquired by practice and a capacity for taking persistent and well-ordered pains.   An angler must never be flurried by the perverseness of the wind, by the untoward tricks which the fly or line will sometimes play, or by the peculiarities of the stream; he cannot overcome these by sheer strength, and he must learn to dodge them and defeat them unobtrusively. Quiet, steady, intelligent effort is needed to become a master of the rod and line, to be able to do with them the best that can be done.

To throw a fly well is one step, and it is essential, but not by itself enough. A habit of attention and observation is at least equally important, and this observation must have a wide range. It must take notice of the ways of fish at all times, especially when feeding and when hooked; of different conditions of weather and water, and of the effect of these, till by degrees the angler will have at his disposal a little individual store, peculiarly his own, of suggestions, hints and probabilities. Things that he watches, or sees happen season by season, come to have meanings, and are signs which suggest expedients as the result of former experience. The attention of an angler must not be a barren but a fertile attention. His observation should add to his knowledge in a manner which has a direct bearing on his sport. He should make guesses founded upon something which he has noticed, and be ever on the watch for some further indications to turn the guess into a conclusion.

We have now arrived at two main qualities—the first being a certain physical cleverness, and the second an attentive and suggestive mind. But there is a third which seems to me important. It is self-control; for if an angler is really keen, he will have many struggles with himself in early days. The greater the keenness the more bitter the disappointment, and the more highly nerves have been strung by excitement the more likely are we to collapse under disaster. And yet it is a pity, and a waste of good things, that the loss of even the biggest fish should make the other pleasures and successes of the day of no account. In angling, as in all other recreations into which excitement enters, we have to be upon our guard, so that we can at any moment throw a weight of self-control into the scale against misfortune, and happily we can study to some purpose, both to increase our pleasure in success and to lessen the distress caused by what goes ill. It is not only in cases of great disasters, however, that the angler needs self-control. He is perpetually called upon to use it to withstand small exasperations. There are times when all small things seem adverse, when the hook is perpetually catching in inanimate objects, when unexpected delays and difficulties of various kinds occur at undesirable moments, when fish will rise short, or when they feed greedily on natural flies, and will not look at artificial ones. These sorts of things tend to hurry and exasperation, which lead certainly to bad fishing, which in turn ends in a small basket and disgust.

People talk sometimes as if a sort of still slow patience were the great quality exercised by angling. It ought much more properly to be called self-control, and if another quality essential to success is to be added, let it be endurance. Hard work and continual effort make a tremendous difference to the basket in fly fishing, and though the amount of strength required for any given cast may not be great, yet eight hours' fishing even with a single-handed trout rod is, if the most be made of the time, a hard day's work.

There is not, it is true, the same glory of physical strength and prowess in angling as in games; but, on the other hand, the skill required is as difficult and various, and can be maintained unimpaired long after the highest point of our physical activity has been reached and passed. When, moreover, as the years go on, reflection and observation begin to take the place of competition, a wider pleasure in angling opens out. The extent to which we appreciate this is, I suppose, again a matter of temperament. It is not everybody who cares for the independence and comparative solitude of angling; and there are probably some people who would consider either of these as a drawback. Nor are we all equally attracted by the charm and changes of the season and by natural beauties, nor all equally interested in the life of the country. The gift of being pleased by these things is one of the most precious possessions that a man can have within him, but it is rare to find it at an early age. In boyhood it is generally dormant, and it is not this that we think of when we first begin to fish; but presently there comes a time when we realize that angling is often taking us to the most beautiful places of the country at the very best times of year, and then we feel a new sense of gratitude and a crowning delight. From now onwards we look at more than the river. There come times when the beauty of the day or of the place seems to possess us, so that the thought of angling ever afterwards becomes full of beautiful associations, of delightful meadows and woods, of light upon water, of the sound of streams, till in the recollection of days that are past, the vision of these things perpetually rises up and fills us with joy. Then there comes the longing, which is intense, to escape and be again among the surroundings that we remember, and we plan to set apart our leisure for angling, partly for its own sake, but partly also because we cannot let the season go by without revisiting chosen places, when we know that spring or summer is there. One thing perhaps should be borne in mind to prevent disappointment, and that is not to ask too much of Nature suddenly, when we have been strained by overwork; at such times we are out of tune, and more fit for rest than for enjoyment. If we are to enter into the moods of Nature, we must bring with us some vigour and elasticity of spirit. A feeble mind looking upon fair scenes with a languid eye will not feel the joy of them, and it is with Nature as with friendship —we cannot take all and bring nothing. On the other hand, work, if it be of an interesting sort and not crushing in amount, is a fine preparation for the country. Such work is stimulating, and when we make our escape we do it with faculties erect and active, with every sense alert and eager for sights and sounds and all joys, which are not to be met with in cities. Then we bring with us such an uprising of the spirit, that we seem to be fit companions for Nature even on her finest and best days in spring.

CHAPTER II

DRY FLY FISHING

It is with much diffidence that any attempt can be made to describe the delights of dry fly fishing. Those who know and practise the art best are the epicures among anglers; they have carried both the skill and pleasure of angling to a height of exquisite refinement, and to them I fear that any detailed account of a day's dry fly fishing must seem inadequate. There are, however, other less fortunate anglers whom circumstances have prevented from becoming acquainted with the use of the dry fly on those rivers which are most perfectly suited for it, and as these anglers are not only many in number, but are probably a very large majority of anglers, I will endeavour to describe some of the days, the events, the places, the rivers, the seasons, which are to me typical of dry fly angling, in the hope of finding readers to whom such things are not already too familiar. If the written words can convey to them even a little of what dry fly angling means to us on the Test and the Itchen, of the affection we feel for these rivers and their water meadows, my object will be gained and my hope fulfilled.

First, let us take the season. Every season has its claim upon the attention of men whose recreations are in the country and in open air, but in the case of the dry fly angler this claim is paramount, for the season which is the very best for the use of the dry fly is also the very best of the whole year. It consists of the months of May and June, when Nature does her utmost on a scale that is magnificent, and with a variety that seems infinite, to persuade us that we live in a beautiful world. The extent to which this appeal, which Nature makes to us, is admitted or felt by different persons, varies within very wide limits. A large number of people leave their homes, and make considerable pecuniary sacrifices, in order apparently to spend the best part of the spring and early summer in London and out of the country. There are others, on the contrary, to whom it is a calamity to be shut up in a town for the whole of the months of May and June; and whom no purely self-regarding misfortune, except perhaps the complete loss of liberty or of health, could make more wretched than this. It is, however, not only the season of the year, but the places for dry fly angling, that add to the attractions of the sport. It would be arrogant to say that the valleys of the Test and Itchen are better than any other part of the country in May and June, but I do say that no part is better than they are. The angler who is fishing in one of these rivers at this time of year, is seeing the most beautiful season at its best. This is the time of blossom and promise, everywhere there should be visible growth responding to increasing warmth, a sense of luxuriant and abundant young life all around us. All this is assured every year in the valleys of such rivers as the Test and the Itchen. There may be, and too often is, a spring drought in other counties, and on the great downs of Hampshire itself. Other rivers may shrink, and leave their banks dry, but the Hampshire chalk streams run brim full,[1] and their valleys are full of water meadows, intersected by streams and runnels and channels and cuts of all sorts and sizes carrying over the land the bounty of water. Hence it is, that on the way to our river we have no thought of what order it will be in, or of what rain there has been lately. The river is sure to be found full and clear. North country rivers are fed by constant tributaries. Down every glen comes a burn, and after heavy rain there is a rush of surface water, which swells them all. A true chalk stream has few tributaries. The valleys on the higher ground near it have no streams; the rain falls upon the great expanse of high exposed downs, and sinks silently into the chalk, till somewhere in a large low valley it rises in constant springs, and a full river starts from them towards the sea. There is always something mysterious to me in looking at these rivers, so little affected by the weather of the moment, fed continually by secret springs, flowing with a sort of swiftness, but for the most part (except close to mills and large hatches) silently, and with water which looks too pure and clear for that of a river of common life.

And now let the season be somewhere about the middle of May, and let there be a holiday, and the angler be at the Test or the Itchen, and let us consider a day's

[1] The volume of water is less after prolonged drought than it is in a wet year, but it varies little from one week to another. In wet years the river if it be a pure chalk stream is never sullied by turbulent floods: in dry years the stream is less strong, but it does not fail, and the river is kept bank high by hatches that are maintained to water the meadows.

fishing, which shall be typical of many days in this month. The wind shall be south-west, a perceptible breeze, but with no squalls or rough manners; and there shall be light clouds moving before it, between which gleams of sunshine fall upon the young leaves and woods —for there are many fine woods by the sides of water meadows. Granted these first two conditions, it will follow that the day is warm, with a temperature reaching 62° in the shade, the mean temperature for midsummer, but a very suitable maximum in the month of May. It is almost certain that there will be a rise of trout at some time during the day, and it is all-important to know at what hour it will begin. The chances in my experience are something as follows: It is not certain that there will be no rise before ten o'clock, but it is very improbable that there will be one. After ten o'clock the rise may begin at any time. The most likely time for it is between eleven and twelve, but there need be no disappointment if it does not begin till twelve o'clock. On a day such as this I do, however, become anxious if at one o'clock there is still no rise. Taking then these chances into consideration, desiring earnestly not to miss a minute of the rise, and leaving a fair margin for uncertainties, the angler will probably be at the water by half-past nine.

If this forecast of the time of the rise proves correct, and there is at first neither fly nor fish to be seen, the angler has at any rate the satisfaction of feeling that the day is all before him, and that he has so far missed nothing. If he is very impatient to have an outlet at once for his energy, he may put on a medium-sized hackle fly and use it wet in the rough water of hatch-holes, but he can do no good—and perhaps he may do some harm—by attempting to fish the river at large. Even in the hatch-holes he will probably prick more fish than he hooks, and if one or two are landed they will either be small trout, or large ones in inferior condition. The fact is, that attempts to anticipate success in a chalk stream before the proper rise begins are unsatisfactory; however resolutely the angler may have made up his mind to expect nothing from these attempts, yet if he labours at them, some sense of disappointment will insensibly steal over him, and take just a little off the edge of his keenness. In my opinion, it is better to keep this unimpaired till the rise begins. It is not hard to wait for an hour or two on such a day; one need only watch and listen to the life about the river. To read a book at this time is not so easy, for the eyes are continually being lifted from its pages to the water. On the other hand, there is not much to be gained by wandering up and down, and the best plan is for the angler to go to the lowest part of the water he means to fish, and there sit down to watch some particular bit of it, which is known to be a good place for free rising trout. The first sign of the coming rise will be a few flies upon the water, either olive duns or some near relations of theirs. These are generally noticed by the angler before the fish begin to take them, but sometimes it is a trout which first notices a fly, and then a rise is the first visible sign. When this is so, the angler becomes alert at once. The pleasure of the day began for him, let us hope, hours ago, when he woke to the consciousness of what sort of day it was; but now there is suddenly added to his happiness the delight of endeavour and excitement, suspense ends, action begins, and hope is raised to the height of expectation. He does not, however, cast at once, but gets quietly within reach, kneeling if necessary to be out of sight, and waiting for the fish to rise again. This first trout should be risen, if it is in a convenient place where the fly does not drag. In a little time it may have made up its mind not to take any flies on the surface, or its appetite may have become less keen, or its sense of what all natural flies look like more exact; but just at first, at the very beginning of the rise, there is most probability of finding it hungry and off its guard. By the time the first fish is done with, it should be easy to find others rising, and if there is a free rise and plenty of fly, the angler will in May get the best conditioned fish in comparatively quick running water in the main stream. The first half-hour will decide what kind of rise there is to be, whether it is to be a good taking one or not: if it is a good one, the angler should feel for the next two hours that there is at any rate a fair chance of his having a rise whenever he can succeed in floating his fly satisfactorily and accurately over a rising trout. Should the rise last as much as four hours, it is a long one and ought to result in an exceptionally heavy basket. I have generally found, however, that in the last hour or so of the rise the trout become very fastidious and particular. Sometimes they can be seen still in their feeding places, keeping close to the surface of the water, but only taking a fly occasionally, and the angler may, till he is weary, float his own fly over them continually and get no response whatever.   As a rule, on a fairly warm day the rise of fly will be over by three or four o'clock.   The trout will by then have disappeared, and the angler may leave off.   Bad luck or good luck may have made the difference of one or two brace to his basket, but ten pounds' weight of trout should make him content, fifteen pounds may be considered very good, and twenty pounds and upwards exceptional.

The number of trout in different parts of the Itchen and Test is in inverse proportion to their weight; but in the parts of these rivers where the trout are not over-crowded and average from a pound and a half to two pounds, they rise freely and their appearance in a good season is splendid.   The extraordinary fatness to which they attain, and the brilliancy of their colour and con-dition in May, June, and July, surpass anything it has been my good fortune to see among river trout, and any-thing I could have believed, if I had fished only in north country rivers.   On the other hand, the chalk stream trout do not fight so strongly in proportion to their size as the trout in rocky or swifter rivers with rougher water and no weeds.   It is not that the southern trout is less strong, but it thinks too much of the weeds: it is always trying to hide itself instead of trying to get free by wild desperate rushes, for which indeed the presence of the weeds and the gentleness of the water make these rivers less suited.   Sometimes the first rush of a chalk stream trout when hooked is as sudden and wild and strong as that of a fish of the same size in any other river; but in my experience this generally happens with a south country trout when its feeding place is far down on a

shallow or in a long mill-tail, and its home is in the
hatch-hole or under the mill above. In such places I
have known a trout of a pound and a half leave very few
yards of line upon the reel before its first rush could be
checked, and the line to be run out as swiftly and as
straight as any one could wish. Twice during the last
season did it happen to me to have fine experiences of
this kind. In the first case the trout had something over
twenty yards to go for safety, and nearly succeeded. Had
the distance been two or three yards less it would have
been accomplished in the first rush, but in the last few
yards the trout had to collect its strength for a second
effort. There was a moment's pause in the impetus of
the rush, and a struggle began in which at first the trout
gained ground, but very slowly, while every foot was
contested with the utmost pressure that I dared put
upon the gut: then there ceased to be progress, and at
last within close sight of its home the trout had to turn
its head. The rest was easy, the mill-tail being fairly
clear of weeds, and both time and stream being against
the fish.

In the second case the result was different. I was
wading in a shallow where I could see the trout, which,
as it turned out, was never to be mine. It was a light-
coloured fish feeding actively and recklessly on the flies,
which were coming down freely, and it took my fly at
once with perfect confidence. It sometimes happens,
however, that these active, reckless, easily hooked trout
are more surprised and desperate when hooked than any
others. I never saw anything more mad and sudden
than the rush of this trout. It gained a pool below some

hatches, where no doubt it lived, and took the line under
the rough main stream into a fine whirling backwater:
then I felt the confusion of having lost touch with the
fish, for there was nothing but the dull sodden strain of a
line hopelessly drowned in the contending currents of
the hatch-hole. The trout jumped high in the middle
of the pool, and showed me that it might be under two
pounds in weight, but was certainly very thick and
strong; I dropped the point of the rod without being
able to give the least relief to the fine gut at the end, and
the stream swept downwards a useless length of submerged line without a fly.

Those anglers who are used to thinking that a day's
fishing means fishing all day, may ask whether it does
not make the pleasure less when the actual fishing is
concentrated into a space of sometimes only two, and
at most four or five hours, as is the case on a chalk
stream in the month of May. The answer is, that the
pleasure and excitement are highly concentrated too, and
that the work while it lasts is very hard. To be using
a small fly and fine gut where there are plenty of large
trout and when there is a good rise, is a glorious experience. Before it is over the angler will have had thrilling
and exciting incidents, enough to provide much reflection, and let us hope satisfaction too, and if the rise
lasted all day we should be apt to miss much of the glory
of the month.

There is so much to be seen and heard in May.
There are the separate and successive greens of the fresh
young leaves of different trees, perhaps the most tender
and the most transient of all the colours that leaves or

flowers give to any season. Then there are the great blossoms of May, of which I especially value six, all so conspicuous in colour as to compel attention, and three of them wonderful in perfume. They are the lilac, hawthorn, gorse, horse-chestnut, laburnum, and broom. Not to spend time in the country while all these things are at their best, is to lead a dull life indeed; and yet, if we are not to miss some of them, we must spend a part at least of every week of May in going about the country with attention free and eyes afield. Dry fly fishing leaves many hours free for this. The first half of May, too, is the most favourable time for making discovery of birds. The summer birds have nearly all arrived, and all birds are singing; but the leaves are not thick yet, and both in brushwood and in trees it is comparatively easy to see the different species. They are active with the business and excitement of the breeding season, and it is just at this time that they most attract the notice of eye and ear. A little later on the air will still be full of sound and song, but it will be much more difficult owing to the leaves to get a good sight of any bird that has attracted attention or raised a doubt of its identity by its song.

May is a good month on a chalk stream, but to my mind the perfection of dry fly fishing is to be had on a good day in mid-June, on water where the May-fly never appears, first to excite the trout and the anglers, and then to leave the fish without appetite and the angler too often discontented. The May-fly is a fine institution, and where it comes in enormous quantities, as it does on some rivers such as the Kennet, which have but a poor rise of duns, it provides a fortnight of most glorious fishing; but elsewhere it interrupts the season, and unless the trout are very large, or there is a great lack of duns and small flies, I would not attempt to re-introduce the May-fly where it has ceased to exist in any numbers.

And now let the pleasure of this June day be heightened by the contrast of work and life in London. This is not the place in which to write of the deep human interests of London, of what great affairs have their centre and of what issues are discussed and decided there. All that follows is written without any thought of denying or minimizing the attraction of these things for men's minds; but there is an aspect of London which is inevitable and becomes most oppressive in hot June days. There is the aggressive stiffness of the buildings, the brutal hardness of the pavement, the smell of the streets festering in the sun, the glare of the light all day striking upon hard substances, and the stuffiness of the heat from which there is no relief at night—for no coolness comes with the evening air, and bedroom windows seem to open into ovens; add to these hardships what is worse than all, the sense of being deprived of the country at this time and shut off from it. Perhaps you own a distant garden, which you know by heart, and from which occasionally leaves and flowers are sent to you in London; you unpack these and spread them out and look at them, spelling out from them and recalling to memory what the garden is like at this time. There were the young beech leaves and the sprays of double flowering cherry in May, and now there come the first out-of-door roses and the first of other things, perhaps the flower of some special iris lately planted. You see these things, you know the very trees, bushes, and places from which they were taken; you know the very form and aspect which the beauty of the season is taking in your garden, and you have the knowledge that it is passing away, that you are missing for all this year things which are dear to you, both for the delight of seeing them afresh each season and for many old associations of other years. At such moments there surges within you a spirit of resentment and indignation, kept in abeyance during the actual hours of hard work, but asserting itself at all other times, and you pass through the streets feeling like an unknown alien, who has no part in the bustle and life of London, and cannot in the place of his exile share what seem to others to be pleasures. Work alone, however interesting, cannot neutralize all this, because it is only partly by the mind that we live. Mental effort is enough for some of the satisfaction of life; but we live also by the affections, and where out-of-door things make to these the irresistible appeal, which they do make to some natures, it is impossible to live in London without great sacrifice. Happily it is possible to go away, if not to home, at any rate to some country retreat at the end of the week, and to combine the best of dry fly fishing with this on Saturday. Where this can be done, the prospect of the escape on Saturday till Monday is a great consolation in all moments of leisure during the week. It is borne about with us like a happy secret; it draws the thoughts towards it continually, as Ruskin says that the luminous distance in a picture attracts the eye, or as the gleam of water attracts it in a landscape.

If our work will let us escape on Friday evening, it is luxury; but even if we belong only to those in the middle state of happiness, who work till midnight or later on Friday, and can have the whole of Saturday and Sunday in the country, we may still be splendidly well off, provided that we are careful to miss nothing. The earliest trains leave Waterloo, the usual place of departure for the Itchen or Test, either at or just before six o'clock in the morning. To leave London it is possible once a week, even after late hours, to get up in time for these early trains, and if you have no luggage (and you need have none if you go to the same place week after week), you will not find it difficult to get to the station. There are places where hansoms can be found even at these hours of the morning; they are not numerous, and they seem quite different from the hansoms that are abroad at more lively hours, but they can be found if you will look for them at certain places. The best plan, however, is to live within a walk of Waterloo, and as you cross the river in the early summer morning, you may feel more reconciled to London than at any other time, and understand Wordsworth's tribute to the sight from Westminster Bridge. I pass over the scene at Waterloo station, which at this hour is very different from the usual one, and the journey, on which perhaps one sleeps a little, though I have found that, while it is very easy to sleep sitting up in the late hours of the evening, it is necessary to lie down, if one wishes to sleep in the early hours of the morning. At some time between eight and nine o'clock, you step out of the train, and are in a few minutes among all the long-desired things. Every sense is alert and every scent and everything seen or heard is noted with delight. You are grateful for the grass on which you walk, even for the soft country dust about your feet.

Let me again be free to choose the day, and let it be bright and cloudless without wind this time. A warm day with a maximum temperature of 75° in the shade; rather trying weather for a wet fly angler, but not at all bad for dry fly fishing at this season, and the sooner the angler can satisfy himself with breakfast and be by the water the better. On such a day in mid-June some fish should be found rising at any time after eight o'clock, and this is said without prejudice to what may happen before eight o'clock, of which I have no experience. There are thirteen hours of daylight after eight o'clock in the morning, and that is enough for a full day's fishing. But the rise will probably be quite different in character to the rise in May. It will be much more prolonged, but more quiet, and the beginning and end of it will not be so clearly defined. You may expect the fish to take best, and you will probably find most fish rising between ten o'clock and two o'clock in the day; but both before and after these hours, there should be some trout feeding. The rise of fish corresponds of course to the rise of fly, and there will probably be some duns upon the water all day, but at no time in such quantities as during the few hours into which the hatching is concentrated earlier in the season and in colder weather. This is what makes June such a good month: the fishing is spread over a much longer period of the day. It is true that the trout are not so greedy, but on the other hand, partly for this very reason and partly because the flies are less numerous at any one time, they are not so likely to do nothing but rush about after *larvæ*, and it is better to be casting over the most fastidious trout which is taking flies on the surface, than over the hungriest one that is " bulging." On a bright warm day such as this, the angler will go very quietly, watching the water, always expecting to see a rise, but knowing that a trout may be well on the feed and yet rising slowly at comparatively long intervals of time. The little light coloured places with a gentle swirl of water immediately below a patch of weed are very favourite spots, and in these it is often possible to see a fish very clearly. On a bright day, the angler should therefore not only look for a rise, but look also for the fish, and many a trout will be discovered lying on the watch for flies before it is actually seen to take one. There is not much difficulty in telling by its attitude in the water, whether a trout is worth trying for. Between the appearance of a trout that is resting motionless and dull upon the bottom, and one that is poised in the water near the surface, there is all the difference in the world; the very attitude of the latter, still as it may be for the moment, seems to have something watchful and lively about it.

In June the trout should be at their very best and strongest, and the angler should be ambitious and go to the water, where he knows there are large fish to match his skill and his fine gut against them in bright weather.

Many a big trout will be seen, risen, and hooked, but the weeds as well as the fish are strong now, and where two-pounders are common and taking well, there are sure to be catastrophes in a long day's fishing. On the other hand, except on very unlucky days, what triumphs there are! what moments of suspense as the fly is floating to the place where one feels sure, either from the sight of the rise or of the very fish itself, that a great trout is feeding! Often in the case of these large trout my rod trembles visibly as the fly comes to the spot, perhaps after all not to be taken. I cannot say which is the more exciting, to have seen only the rise, or to be watching the movement of the fish. The crisis of the rise at one's own fly comes more suddenly when the body of the trout is unseen, but when the fish itself is visible there is a tremendous instant of expectation, as he is seen to prepare to take the fly. The next feeling with me is generally one of downright fear as to where the first rush of the fish will end. This rush may have nothing deliberate about it, in which case all may go well, and in a few seconds the angler may be on equal terms with the fish, and before a minute is over fighting with the odds on his side. On the other hand, there may be in the first rush a horrible set purpose, on the part of the trout, to gain some root under the bank, or to plunge far into a thick bed of weeds, in which case the angler is likely to have the worst of it, for during the first few seconds after being hooked any good conditioned trout of two pounds or upwards can be the master of fine gut. Nor is fine gut the only difficulty: there is another risk owing to the smallness of the hook. It may be possible to succeed with a fairly large imitation of an olive dun on dark days early in the season, but on these days in June a rather small red quill will be the best fly. A small fly, if it is to float well, must be tied on a small hook, and a small hook, unless it should fasten in an extra tough part of the mouth, can have but a weak hold of the fish. The angler must therefore be prepared to lose a large fish every now and then—oftener probably than he thinks quite consistent with good luck—by the hook losing its hold. In this matter of losing fish we are more at the mercy of luck in June than in May, and there are times when the luck seems so bad as to turn what promises to be a record day into a comparatively poor one. Sometimes this luck comes in runs. I remember on one day in the height of the summer having, with small red quills and fine gut, the best and the worst luck combined. There were not great numbers of fish feeding, and the trout that were rising were not rising fast. It took a little patience to find a rising fish, and then more patience to fix its exact position by waiting for its next rise. When these things were discovered, however, each fish took my fly confidently, and it seemed as if only the biggest and fattest trout were rising. With each of the first seven fish hooked there was a moment when a catastrophe seemed imminent, and yet all were landed. They averaged just over two pounds apiece, and after each one the sense of triumph and success mounted higher, till it produced a feeling of confidence in my own skill and luck, which I knew was not justified, but which was irresistible. Then everything changed and one disaster succeeded another. I lost more than seven large trout successively. Some broke my tackle, in the case of others the small hook lost its hold unexpectedly, whilst others again went into weeds and there freed themselves from the hook. Indeed I had a very bad time all round. At the end of the rise my basket was heavy, but I had a sense of being much chastened, and I could have wished that the luck had been more evenly distributed.

After two o'clock on this June day the angler will probably find that it becomes increasingly difficult to find a rising trout, and that when one is found, it is not nearly so ready to take his fly. By working hard all the afternoon he may add a brace more to his basket, and he must decide for himself whether this extra brace is worth two or three hours of watching and walking and crawling and kneeling and effort. If he has done pretty well by two o'clock, and if the rise has then become very slack, he may find it more pleasant to leave off for a few hours and arrange the rest of his day so as to come fresh and strong and keen to the evening rise. One difficulty about the evening rise is to settle the time for dining. After various experiments I have found it best to have dinner, if possible, between five and six o'clock. Two conditions are essential for this: one is, that there should be some place near the river where dinner can be had, and the other, that the angler should not have eaten much luncheon. The latter of these conditions is not only always possible, but easy out of doors: the former one is generally present on the Itchen or Test, where numerous villages with inns are to be found all along the river valleys. Having dined, the angler can call the whole of

the long June evening his own, and may enjoy that sense
of perfect freedom, strength and patience which is so
valuable, and which in fishing is destroyed by hunger or
the thought of a fixed dinner hour ahead.

I must own that I do not appreciate the evening rise
so well as that in the morning; and there are various
reasons for this. In the first place, there is a more
definite limit to the end of the evening rise. It is often
nearly eight o'clock when it begins, and you know then
that the light cannot last for more than an hour. Now
part of the charm of the morning rise is the prospect of
indefinite length. It may only last a short time, but it
may go on for hours, and you feel at the beginning that
its possibilities are unknown. There is nothing of this
with a late evening rise. On the contrary, you feel in a
hurry because the time must be short. If a rising trout
will not take your fly, you begin to fidget as to whether
it will be better to stick to that fish or to try another, and
if half an hour passes without any success, the threat of
an absolutely blank evening makes itself felt. There is
a story of a thrifty and anxious housewife, who used to
call her household early on Monday mornings in terms
like these, " Get up! get up at once! to-day's Monday,
to-morrow's Tuesday, next day's Wednesday, here's half
the week gone and no work done!" It is some such
fidgety anxiety that comes over me, if I do not get a fish
soon in the evening rise. I seem to have the anticipation of complete failure. The time is so short; the
beginning and the end of the rise are so near together,
that failure in the first part seems a presage of failure
in the whole.

The *look* of the evening rise is so often the best of it. Numbers of trout appear to be rising frequently and steadily and confidently, but when the angler puts them to the test, they disappoint him. On some evenings the trout cease to rise after an artificial fly has once been floated over them; on others they continue to rise freely, but will take nothing artificial, and the angler exhausts himself in efforts and changes of fly, working harder and more rapidly as he becomes conscious of the approaching end of the day.

But all evenings are not alike disappointing, and on a warm still evening in June we may expect some success. A few fish may be found rising very quietly and unobtrusively at any time after six o'clock. The angler will probably find that these trout are not feeding in the same way as they fed in the morning. They may be the same fish, but their manners and behaviour are different. They are apparently taking some very small insect, are much more easily scared, and are apt to rise very short, if they rise at all to an artificial fly; still they are feeding, and are worth trying for. If the angler can get one or two of these fish before eight o'clock he will have done well. Soon after eight the evening rise proper should have begun. More rises will be seen than at any previous time of the day, and as the light fades the easier it is to get near the fish, and the more chance is there of hooking them. Yet in my experience it is comparatively seldom that one has a really successful evening, and feels that everything has gone well. Now and then one gets two or three brace, or even more, of good trout, but more often, either because the trout rise short, or because too much time is spent unsuccessfully over a stubborn fish, the angler seems to be always on the point of great success without attaining it.

Anglers differ as to how late the evening fishing should be prolonged. Night fishing with a large wet fly should not be allowed on good dry fly water. It is poor fun to haul out of the river by main force in the dark, on thick gut, a trout that might give good sport in daylight. Before it gets dark, however, there is a half-hour in which it is just possible to see where a fish is rising, but just not possible to see one's fly. It needs both skill and judgment to put an artificial fly properly over a fish in these conditions, but during this half-hour a skilful angler may expect to get a brace of good trout with a floating sedge fly. This is perfectly fair fishing, but it has not the same interest as the finer fishing in better light; it needs skill, and yet it is comparatively clumsy work. The angler strikes at sight of a rise without being sure whether it is to his fly or not. He can, and indeed must, use stronger gut, because, when a trout is hooked, he cannot tell accurately what it is doing, or follow its movements adjusting the strain carefully to the need of each moment as he would do in daylight. In short a great part of all that happens, both before and after he hooks a trout, is hidden from him, and he has in the end to rely more upon force, and less upon skill, to land the fish. All this takes away much of the pleasure, and if the day has been a fairly good one, I would rather forego the last brace than kill them under inferior conditions. On the other hand, if luck has been very bad, or the trout have been particularly exasperating and successful in defeating the angler, or have refused to rise all day, then the sedge fly in the last half-hour of perceptible twilight gives a very satisfactory opportunity of trying to get even with them. After a fair day, however, it seems to me better to leave off when I cease to be able to see a medium-sized quill gnat upon the water at a reasonable distance.

Very pleasant the evening is after a successful day in hot, bright weather in June. Let us suppose that the angler has caught some three brace of trout in the day, and a brace and a half in the evening on good water. He will then have had plenty of interest and excitement, moments of anxiety and even of disappointment, but all contributing at the end to give a delightful satisfactory feeling of successful effort. Some great events, some angling crisis there will have been during the day, to which his thoughts will recur often involuntarily. Some incidents will seem to have been photographed upon his mind, so that he can recall clearly not only the particular things done or seen, but his own sensation at the time. What he thinks about in the evening will not be only of angling, but of the scenes in which he has spent the day. I am often ashamed to think how much passes unnoticed in the actual excitement of angling, but the general impression of light and colour, and surroundings is not lost; some is noted at the time, and some sinks into one's mind unconsciously and is found there at the end of the day, like a blessing given by great bounty to one who was too careless at the time to deserve it. May is the month of fresh leaves and bright shrubs, but June is the month in which the water meadows themselves

"Yellow Iris, Ragged Robin, and Forget-me-not make rough
damp places gay"
(see p. 47)

are brightest. The common yellow iris, ragged robin, and forget-me-not make rough damp places gay, and the clear water in the little runnels among the grass sparkle in the sun. Of wild shrubs which flower in June, there are two so common that they seem to possess the month and meet the eye everywhere. One is the wild rose, and the other is the elder, and great is the contrast between them. The commonest sort of wild rose is surely the most delicate of all shrubs in spite of its thorns. It is exquisitely delicate in the scent, colour, form, and character of its flowers, and there is nothing more graceful in nature than the way in which a long spray of wild rose in full blossom offers its beauty to be admired. I am not so fond of the elder; when one is close to it there is a certain stiff thickness about the bush, and a deadness of colour both of leaves and flowers, and the scent is heavy and spiritless. But masses of elder flower at a distance have a fine foamy appearance, and I always feel that they are doing their best to honour the season. Though the sun may be as hot as midsummer, everything in the first half of June seems young and fresh and active. Birds are singing still, and for a week or two it seems as if the best of spring and summer, warmth and songs, luxuriance and freshness, were spread abroad so abundantly that it is almost too much. The cup of happiness is full and runs over. Such may be one's last thoughts in the quiet of approaching night after sounds have ceased, and in the perfect enjoyment of "that still spirit shed from evening air."

As June draws to a close, and during the whole of

July, the rise during the day becomes more uncertain and feeble. There are many days in July when the dry fly angler spends more time in watching and waiting than in active fishing. His best chance before the evening will be between ten and one o'clock, and though he must be prepared for very light baskets, yet there are mornings in July when trout are to be found feeding slowly and quietly here and there, and when they will take a red quill gnat if it is put to them attractively. I have known days in July when the result of a morning's fishing has been unexpectedly good, equal in total weight to that of the very best days in other months, and equal also in regard to the size and condition of the individual fish.

In August I have only once had a morning's fishing which could fairly be compared, as regards the total weight of trout landed, with the good days of earlier months, and it always seems to me that the condition of the trout in this month ceases to be quite first-rate. Of September, on dry fly rivers, I have had no experience. Anglers who write of it agree in saying that the trout rise better, but that their condition has fallen off, and that an unduly large proportion of female fish are killed.

CHAPTER III

DRY FLY FISHING (*continued*)

ANGLERS who desire to learn the art of dry fly fishing should read and study such a book as *Dry Fly Fishing in Theory and Practice*, by Mr. F. M. Halford. I do not for a moment pretend to be able to give instruction of value and completeness equal to that contained in Mr. Halford's book, and still less to improve upon it; but there is so much variety in angling and in individuals that each record of personal experience has something new, which may be interesting and perhaps even suggestive or useful to others. The difficulties of dry fly fishing are common to us all, but we do not all deal with them in the same way. We make various experiments of our own, and each of us after some years of experience has a little store of conclusions which he believes in and endeavours to apply. Some of these conclusions may seem to other anglers to be mere foolishness, but wherever they have been applied for years with moderate success, they are worthy of record. I have, however, at various times started in my own mind so many theories which have been suggested by experience and afterwards upset by it, that I do not desire to press any one to accept an opinion, unless there is anything in his own experience which goes to support it. There is only one theory about angling in which I have perfect confidence, and this is that the two words, least appropriate to any statement about it, are the words "always" and "never." Theories, rules, creeds, and hypotheses are constantly forming in the angler's mind. Trout seem to make it their object to suggest these only to upset and destroy them.

There are three successive objects before the angler: the first is to rise a trout, the second to hook it, and the third to land it. All are essential, but the first is the most important, and in dry fly fishing the most interesting. To achieve the first of these objects the angler tries to make sure, (1) that the trout shall see his fly bearing the greatest possible resemblance to a natural fly in appearance, position, and motion; and (2) that the trout shall see nothing of the angler's person and nothing else of his tackle save the fly. The effort, in short, is to make the trout notice the fly without noticing anything else. It is in this that the fine art of dry fly fishing consists. The fly is a tiny insignificant thing, the angler with his apparatus is more or less bulky and obvious; but he has to display the insignificant and conceal the obvious. This, however, does not explain more than half the difficulty, for the fly which is so small must not only conceal a hook, but also support the weight of the hook and float on the surface of the water, and must do this without any appearance of effort; a fly lying on its side as if tired by the weight of the hook is not nearly so attractive as one sitting upright. In fact, the fly must float as if it were buoyant, cheerful, and in the best of spirits—natural flies having the appearance of being very frivolous and light-hearted. Even now there is more to be said, for the fly must float as if it were unattached to a comparatively heavy line, some yards of which are lying upon the water; and to this it must be added that the fly must float with perfect accuracy to the exact spot where one particular trout has been seen to rise some moments before. In good dry fly water trout are extremely quick to mark anything that is amiss, so that all these matters must be attended to.

The various positions in which a trout may be rising, fall roughly under two heads. The first includes every position under or near the angler's own bank; the second includes any position near the middle or on the opposite side of the stream, though in a very narrow stream all positions may be regarded as coming under the first head. A trout under or near the angler's own bank must as a rule be given the chance of seeing the gut before it sees the fly. If the trout's body is clearly visible in the water, it may be possible in theory to make the fly alight at just such a spot over its head that it can see the fly and nothing else, but I doubt its being possible in practice, for it must be a matter almost of hundredths of an inch, and the angler had better make up his mind that the gut *must* float over the trout first, and make his plans accordingly. If the trout is rising close under the bank and directly in a line above me, I have found the better plan to be to make the fly alight only a few inches above it: in this position some of the gut must not only float, but fall directly over the trout, and it is better that only the finest of the gut should do so. Sometimes a trout is attracted by seeing the fly

actually alight upon the surface, but personally I do not
think it is advisable to pitch the fly as a rule very close
to the fish, and however lightly the cast may be made, I
would rather that the fish did not notice the fly at all, till
it arrives before him floating without motion of its own
upon the surface.

   If the trout is not close under the bank, but only near
to it with a space of open water between, it is better to
throw the fly a yard or more up stream, sometimes two
yards above is not too much, for the farther the fly is
cast with a slanting line above the trout, the less near to
its head does any portion of the gut fall.   There are
days, however, when with all these precautions trout
will not stand the sight of gut, and if so, as a last resort
the angler must try to float his fly down stream over fish
in these positions.   A whole chapter might be written
on the drawbacks to this particular method.   It is
necessary first to make an ugly slack cast, but so that the
fly falls free at the end, and floats in a direct line above
the fish; then the angler, by lowering the point of his
rod and crawling along the bank, does his utmost to
ease the line down stream and to prevent it from dragging the fly back.   If everything goes well there is a
really good chance of a rise, but also a good chance of
the hook being pulled straight out of the fish's mouth
when the strike is made.   Sometimes very shy trout are
caught by this method, but sometimes they do not rise
to the first cast, or the fly floats rather to one side of
them, and then all is over.   When once the fly is past
the trout, there is nothing left for the angler to do, but
to scare the trout by dragging the fly and gut up stream

over its head in the most unnatural manner. This, however, applies only to trout that are rising in a direct line below the angler; with others there are modifications of the down stream method which are possible and more satisfactory, and which I think are too much neglected. It is obvious that with all its drawbacks the down stream method has this advantage, that the fish sees the fly before the gut, and when the angler is casting to a fish under the opposite bank, or on the farther side of a fairly broad stream, he should use as much of the down stream method as he can. By kneeling down as far back from the edge of the bank as possible, the angler can get opposite or nearly opposite to such fish without frightening them, and if having done this, he can make a cast so that the last foot or more of gut with the fly at the end of it is curved down stream, while the body of the line is either straight or convex across the stream, he will have combined the advantages of the down stream method, and at the same time have got rid of its drawbacks. It must be admitted that it is not possible to make sure of this cast, but it is surprising how often it can be done with success, especially if there is a light wind down stream. There is one corner known to me on the Itchen, where good trout are constantly rising under the farther bank. The corner receives in consequence special attention from every one who fishes there. The stream here is slow and smooth, and the fish become very shy: so much so, that it is on many days very difficult to cast over them at all without putting them down. I have noticed at this place that whenever conditions are favourable for arranging the drift of the fly in the manner just described, the chance of rising one of these fish is very much improved, and on still days in the summer it is seldom that I can get a rise from one of them in any other way.

The choice of the fly to be used precedes the making of the cast in point of time, but is second to it in importance. It is better to throw and float the wrong fly really well than to bungle with the right one. In common with most anglers I carry about with me a much larger variety of flies than I ever use, but successive seasons tend to diminish the number rather than to add to it, and in practice I should be content (exclusive of the May-fly and sedge-fly, which are for special waters or exceptional occasions) with four sorts. In May these would be a medium-coloured olive quill gnat, neither very light nor very dark, and the iron blue. The first of these is the one for general use, but the latter is essential also. As a rule, if the rising trout in May will not have the olive quill, the angler will not have very much success with anything else, and he will find that the trout are either bulging or in some state of preternatural suspicion. But there are times when the iron blue comes on the water and is taken, to the exclusion of the other flies. On such occasions the angler will easily notice the presence of iron blues, and change his fly. Sometimes it happens that the trout begin rising at olives, and the iron blue comes up later on. I have notes of days when this has happened, and when the olive was quite satisfactory for the first hour or so of the rise, till the iron blue appeared; after which the olive failed, and an imitation of the iron blue succeeded, though natural olive duns as well as iron blues continued in numbers on the water.

In June, or perhaps even in the end of May, a red quill becomes the more successful fly, and a medium size, neither large nor small, is the best. The trout have a tendency to prefer the smaller sizes, and when their appetite has become very delicate in hot summer weather the smallest possible size [1] of red quill, not the smallest usually offered for sale in tackle shops, but one specially tied on the smallest hooks of all, is the most attractive. This size may do very well with trout up to one pound or one pound and a half, but the hook is too small to hold strong fish of a large size. The big fish lost after being hooked on these tiny flies exceed in numbers those which are landed, and it is better to rise fewer fish with a medium-sized fly than to hook and scare the best ones without getting any of them. The same objection applies to imitations of that troublesome little insect the "curse."

The fourth kind of fly is a plain black hackle, tied with *soft* hackles, and on the same sized hook as the duns. It is always worth while to float this over an obstinate trout, and on many days at all seasons it has taken one or two brace of trout, which I am convinced I should not have succeeded in rising with the winged flies. There are occasions when the black hackle will take trout one after the other. I have a note of one evening, June 16, 1894, after the trout had taken a red quill well in the day-time. I had left off about two

[1] i.e. No. ooo.

o'clock, and returned to the same meadow about six o'clock. The fish were rising again, but very quietly, and they persistently disregarded the same red quills that had been successful before. The black hackle was offered to them dry, and six fish were landed with it. One cannot of course expect the same success with this fly on every evening, but on many evenings, when the trout have been rising in their quiet evening way between six and eight o'clock, I have found the black hackle used dry better than any other fly.

I once had a remarkable experience with this fly. It was on July 16, 1894. There was very little rise in the morning; a few fish were seen, but as each one only rose about once in ten minutes, fishing with the dry fly was very intermittent, and up till one o'clock nothing had been landed. It seemed that nothing more was to be done, and I sat gazing listlessly at the water. A fairly broad straight bit of river was before me, smooth in places, but with small ripples of stream here and there. The thoughts of other rivers and of salmon fishing came into my mind, till at last in a state of sheer despair and idleness it occurred to me that I would try a wet fly, and in salmon-fishing phrase "put it over" the piece of water before me. The black hackle, a very favourite north country fly, was chosen and used as a salmon fly, that is to say it was cast across and down the stream at an angle and kept moving gently, till the action of the stream brought it round to my own bank. The trout took it like salmon take a fly, sometimes under water, sometimes with a fair head and tail rise, sometimes with a plunge, but for the most part either when the fly was midway across the stream, or when it had come well round and was nearly straight below me; and the fish that rose took firm hold, hardly any being lost or only pricked. Now and then an isolated rise would be seen some way below me, and when the place was reached the fish nearly always came up well to the wet black hackle. At three o'clock I had six trout, and four more were added in the same way during the evening rise. The weather was not exceptional, being an ordinary fine summer's day with only a little breeze, some clouds, and intervals of sunlight. The part of the river in which this method had succeeded was not a hatch-hole or any exceptional place of that kind, but a clear, steady, even-flowing, well-fished stretch of the Itchen. It seemed that a great discovery had been made, and that the only difficulty was how to use it with moderation henceforth. Anglers are sanguine men, and are easily transported by unexpected success to heights of confidence; so they will, I trust, sympathize with my simplicity. I have on many occasions tried this fly in the same manner, in the same water, at the same time and also at different times of the season since, but never again has it succeeded to anything like the same extent. Perhaps in some seasons, when the yearly rainfall has ceased to be deficient, when this oppressive series of droughts has come to an end, and chalk streams are flowing strong, full, and clear above the weeds in midsummer, there may come another day such as July 16, 1894; but for the present I have ceased using the black hackle as a wet fly on chalk streams, not because it catches too many trout, but because it catches hardly any, and its record is classed

in my mind with that of " Single-speech Hamilton,"
The Lost Chord, and other illustrations of amazing and
isolated success.

To hook a trout which has risen to a floating fly, it
is necessary to *strike*, for the simple reason that a fish
cannot be hooked on a slack line, and that it is impossible to float a fly naturally without allowing the line
a certain degree of slackness. The line may be straight
upon the water, but a floating fly cannot be kept in
touch with the point of the rod in the same way as a wet
fly, which is being jerked through the water or being
swept round at the end of a line kept extended by the
stream. The rise of a trout is sometimes described as
though the fish took the fly with a dash from below, and
then turned sharply down and hooked itself by its own
weight. This may be so with a wet fly moving under
water, but it is as a rule not the way in which a large
chalk stream trout feeds. It lies close to the surface of
the water, and takes by preference the flies which pass
exactly over it, taking them with the smallest possible
effort and change of position; often it does little more
than just put the end of its mouth to the surface and
withdraw it, taking the fly with the mere tip of the
lips, and rejecting it instantly if it is not what it
expects. It seems to me better therefore (though
authorities differ about this) to strike directly the fly is
seen to be taken. There must in every case be a perceptible interval required to overcome the slackness of
the line before the strike takes effect, and where, as often
happens, the line owing to the manner of the cast or the
action of the stream is not perfectly straight upon or in

the water at the time, this interval is sometimes too long rather than too short.   Large trout, which have probably had some previous education, are apt to feed very carefully and to take the fly so delicately, that the angler often has only half a chance of hooking them at all, and that only at the exact moment when the lips close upon the fly.   Any angler may notice how many of his large trout are hooked in the very edge of the mouth.   I have sometimes, when I could see the fish in the water, intentionally abstained from striking in order to see what happened, and the result has been that, though very small and innocent trout have sometimes taken the fly with a confident gulp, and have had apparently a little difficulty in expelling it under water afterwards, the larger trout have rejected it in an instant.   Where, however, the movement of a trout can be watched in the water, great care is needed to avoid striking too soon; for if the approach and opening of the trout's mouth—the sure signs that it is going to take the fly—are mistaken for the fact of its actually having done so, the trout will certainly be missed and probably be scared.

The art in striking is to use the greatest amount of quickness and decision that can be combined with gentleness; personally I prefer to strike with the hand upon the line, rather than to be dependent upon the nice adjustment of resistance in the reel; and whatever may have been the case in early and more excitable days, I do not find much difficulty now in preventing myself from striking too hard.   But nothing is more annoying than to lose a good trout by striking too hard; the fish then often gives a heavy plunge in surprise and alarm, which increases the idea of its size, and the angler overwhelms himself in consequence with bitter self-reproach. When the gut does break it is generally at the knot which holds the fly, and to guard against this misfortune there are two precautions which no angler can impress upon himself too much. The first is, to soak the end of gut well, not merely at the beginning of the day, but also on every occasion before tying on a new fly; without doing this he cannot be sure of tying a sound knot. The second is, to examine the gut at the head of the fly carefully from time to time. Sooner or later the constant flicking will weaken fine gut, even when the smallest flies are used. Sometimes the gut at the head of the fly becomes untrustworthy in five minutes; sometimes it lasts a long time unimpaired. The length of time for which the gut lasts depends upon the angler's manner of casting and drying his fly, which in its turn will vary with the position of different fish and the angle of the wind. In old days before the use of eyed hooks this weakening of the gut at the head of the fly was a real nuisance; on some days fly after fly had to be thrown away (if it was not actually whipped off) after a little use, but now it is an easy matter to tie the fly on again. It should, however, be remembered that a new fly is more perfect in shape and more attractive than one which has had much whipping to and fro, and, where trout are large and shy, it is better to put on a new fly pretty frequently, and to do so always after landing a fish.

The moment after hooking any trout of two pounds' weight or upwards is generally one of great anxiety. Sometimes the fish pulls steadily from the first, but one in really fine condition generally goes off with a rush, as if it realized in a flash the full horror of the mistake it had made. Fine gut cannot stop such a trout at first, and all the angler can do is to handicap the fish by putting on as much strain as he dare. This is the great crisis: the rise, the strike, and the rush succeed each other in a moment, and the angler's emotions are an exquisite blend of joy and fear. If the trout is clearly making for a bed of weeds it is best to let it go in rather than to risk a break: if it is lightly hooked it will free itself from the fly in the weeds, but it may do this in any case. On the other hand, if the trout is firmly hooked, it is surprising how often the angler is able to extricate his fish by lowering the point of his rod, keeping the line tight and working it gently with his hand. Time after time I have known fish, apparently buried in weeds, be perfectly immovable by the strain of the rod and give no sign of feeling it, and yet become restless and yield to the direct play of the hand upon the reel line. It is, of course, essential that the strain should be applied from *below the weeds*. It is, in my opinion, an error to suppose that the idea of a trout is to roll itself up in weeds and thus to offer resistance: its first object is probably shelter out of sight, but a trout's method of resisting in weeds is, I am convinced, to lay hold of them with its mouth. For years I had noticed that there were generally pieces of weed actually in the mouth of fish that were landed after being hung up in weeds, but it seemed to me unlikely that they really seized the weed with their mouths deliberately. One day, however, I happened to be playing a trout on a clear shallow, where there were no large patches of weed, and where every movement could be seen: the fish came near a small piece of weed and stuck there, and the strain on the rod became that of a dead weight. The thing looked absurd, for the weed was much too small to conceal the fish, and only the head was in contact with it. There was nothing but this ridiculous little bit of weed and the trout—a fish of not much over a pound—and yet I could not move it! When the fish was landed, there as usual was some weed inside the mouth. It will of course occur to any one as a possible explanation (and so it did to me), that the line may have got round the little bit of weed, and so caused the feeling of pulling at a dead weight; but it appeared to me at the time that this was not so, and subsequent experiences of the same kind in shallow water, where I have been wading close to the fish, and have been able to examine the situation at leisure in every detail, have convinced me that trout do attempt to resist the strain of the tackle in the way described.

Weeds are the great and universal difficulty with chalk stream trout, and there are times when large fish break the gut by carrying the line right through patches of them, and so arranging matters that the fish and not the angler settle how much strain the gut has to bear, but on the whole, considering how many and how thick the weeds are, less fish are lost than might be supposed. Trout differ very much in the use they attempt to make of weeds, and every now and then a good fish will appear to neglect the weeds altogether, as if it were too chivalrous to take so great an advantage of the angler. When a fish is bent on doing some quite fatal thing, such as going down through a hatch, the angler must decide, according to his idea of the strength of his tackle and of the size of the fish, whether he had not better at all costs have the fight out then and there and risk being broken at once. He should make up his mind quite clearly about this, and if he thinks he cannot possibly hold the fish by force, he had better slacken the line. The sudden freedom from the strain sometimes changes the intention or tactics of the trout.

I suppose that nowhere else, and never before, have so many large fish been caught on such fine tackle and small hooks, as have been caught on the best dry fly rivers in recent years, and the anglers who fish these rivers know very well that directly a trout is hooked no possible advantage must be neglected. The chief point is to keep below the fish, and fight always with the stream helping you, and not helping the fish. After the first few moments, you should be able with skill and care, first to guide and then control any trout up to three pounds' weight, if you work steadily down stream with it. There is no need for hurry, for time is then on the angler's side, but there comes a point at which the landing net should be got ready for possible chances. A moment of apparent exhaustion generally seizes a trout before it is really exhausted, and if this happens when the fish is within reach it is well to take the opportunity of landing it. On the other hand, at the actual moment of getting the net off the strap, the angler may be taken at a disadvantage, and he should not expose himself to this risk till he is pretty sure that the trout is no longer capable of anything very sudden or violent.

With a very large fish—the thought of losing which is really dreadful—I always have a secret fear of getting the net ready too soon, lest the act should be noticed by some unseen influence, and treated as a sign of that pride which deserves a fall. No attempt should be made to net a good fish till it has turned on its side, and ceased to struggle or splash, and till the net is right under it. The best way is to draw the fish over the net, not to push the net under the fish. In practice there is often a combination of both these movements, but the net should be kept as still and unobtrusive as possible, until the final act of lifting, or rather receiving and drawing the body of the fish to land, and this should be steady, even, and certain. I prefer, being right handed, to keep the rod in the right hand, because the management of the fish with the rod is more difficult and delicate, even at the last moment, than the act of netting.

The dry fly angler on chalk streams has less reason to pay attention to the weather than any other. To those who fish for trout on north country rivers, still more to those who fish for sea trout or salmon, there comes a certain day or days after rain when the rivers are in such perfect order, and when the chance of a very good day's fishing is so excellent, that it is really imperative to take advantage of it; but on the chalk streams of Hampshire this is not so. The rivers are always clear and in order as far as the water is concerned. It is true that the springs which feed them have been seriously diminished by successive droughts and deficiencies of rainfall since the beginning of the summer of 1887, but the system of hatches and mills maintains the level of water at any rate in some meadows, even when the flow of water is lessened, and no amount of rain has a sudden effect upon the condition of these rivers.   The main difficulty of the dry fly angler is with the wind, and he devotes all his efforts to making himself independent of it.   A stiff rod, a fairly heavy line, a short length of gut, and the underhand cast will do wonders in the teeth even of a strong wind; but the dry fly angler cannot compromise with the wind, and if it is down stream he must face it and do his best.   It happens from the nature of things that the cold spring winds blow down stream in the valleys of the Itchen and Test.   These winds in the early part of the season seem to delay the hatch of fly without in the least impairing it: on the contrary, the best hatches of fly and rises of trout often take place in a cold east wind and on a dull, cheerless day.   Sometimes the hatch of flies is delayed till well into the afternoon, but never in May, however cold the wind, need the angler despair of having a really good basket.   On the other hand, I have sometimes in warm weather in May seen the hatch of flies weak and the rise of trout soon over. It is not always so, and I do not mean to say that a cold day and a down stream wind are to be wished for, but only that the angler, who starts on such days with a feeling of disappointment, will often get far more consolation than he expects.   One piece of advice may be given to all anglers, who begin dry fly fishing when they are young, and that is to make themselves ambidextrous, to be able to cast with the left hand as well as with the right.   To my great regret I can only use a single-handed rod with the right hand, but I have seen one man, at least, who could use either hand equally well, and the advantage of being able to use the left hand when fishing up the left bank of a river against the wind is enormous.

On any day in May and June there will almost certainly be some sort of a rise at some time of the day, but rises are of all sorts. Some of the best seeming rises are the most disappointing, and some of those which seem poor turn out to be good taking ones. Whatever the kind of rise may be, it is well to bear in mind that there are some trout which seem to be set as decoys in certain places to attract the angler's attention and make him waste his time. These trout begin to rise soon and leave off late, and refuse to take an artificial fly. The angler who knows the water well, probably knows most of these fish or the places which they frequent, and does not spend much time over them, if there are other fish feeding; but on strange water it is well to be on the lookout for this class of fish, and not to spend too much time over an obstinate trout unless the extent of water at one's disposal is very limited. In the water at Winchester all the trout were more or less of this class, but that was exceptional. On days when the trout are feeding, but ignore the artificial fly, it is best to give special attention to trout in difficult situations, where they are likely to be not so well educated; and if even these are obstinate, the angler had better settle down where most trout are feeding, and stick to them doggedly, changing his fly as often as he likes. A trout which continues to feed will make a mistake sooner or later, if the angler's patience and his wrist and arm hold out long enough. "Bulging" trout in particular are generally not shy, and will stand any amount of fair fishing without ceasing to feed.

The days when I have had most difficulty with the shyness of trout have not been at all bright days, but quiet dull days with an even monotonous light. In this light, and in the evening light before sunset, the trout are often very shy, both of the angler and the gut. Trout differ very much in this respect on different days, and on all days individual trout differ more or less from each other.

A great deal may be learnt of the behaviour of trout on bright days, when they can be seen in the water. Let us suppose that a good fish is seen feeding where the angler can get into position and prepare to cast without disturbing it. The fly is thrown above the trout, which may of course take fright at once and rush off to its shelter, and if so there is an end; but short of this the trout may drop slowly down stream and go quietly away, or may just sink in the water and cease feeding. Assuming, however, that the trout takes no offence at the first cast, it may then take the fly with hesitation, as if it were making an experiment, or with confidence, as if the fly were exactly like a natural one, or with an appearance of rapture, as if the angler's fly were the one thing for which it had been waiting; or finally, the trout may take a middle course between the two possible extremes of fear and confidence, and either take no notice whatever of the fly or move to it and refuse it. It is desperate work to continue to cast over a fish which never takes any notice, but as long as a trout makes any movement towards the fly it is worth while to go on fishing for it

and to try a change of fly. Sometimes a new fly of the
same pattern will succeed where a much used one has
failed, and a change of the size of fly may be as important
as a change of pattern. Now and then the trout is so
interested in the fly that it leaves its place and comes
down stream, inspecting the fly closely as it floats:
sometimes this ends in the trout taking the fly, at others
in its coming down stream till it sees the angler.
Occasionally it neither sees him nor takes the fly and
goes slowly back to its feeding place; and in any case
the angler's only chance is to keep perfectly still and
make no movement, unless the fly is actually taken.

Most trout are scared by rising at an artificial fly, even
when they are not touched by the hook. They know
when you strike that something has happened, which
they did not expect, and they either cease feeding or
refuse for some time to rise to the artificial fly again.
On the other hand, I have occasionally been clearly
conscious of touching a trout in striking, and seen it
continue to rise afterwards. With one trout I had a
curious experience—it was a fish of at least two pounds'
weight and apparently in very good condition. It rose
to my fly at the first cast; I struck, and for a just perceptible moment the rod bent, and I thought I had the
trout, but the fly came back to me, and I saw the fish
drop down stream and lie at the bottom, apparently
meditative rather than frightened. Very soon it began
to work up stream, and in a few minutes was rising again
in the same place as before. Again I made what seemed
to me a cast much like the first one, but this time it had
the effect of putting the trout down altogether. On

"The fly came back to me"

more than one subsequent day in the same season, though there was a fish, which I believe to be the identical one referred to above rising in that spot, I never could get a rise from it, and it generally disappeared at the first cast. I have given this instance of an individual trout having found safety in education, because on the first occasion I never for a moment lost sight of the fish, and could be sure of its identity during the whole time. There would otherwise have been no certainty of its being the same fish that rose a second time in the same place on the first day. It is astonishing how soon the exact position of one rising trout will be taken by another as soon as there is a vacancy: sometimes if the angler gets a trout quickly down stream after hooking it, he may on returning to the place after the first trout has been landed, find a second already occupying the vacant place and feeding there, as if it had known the advantages of this particular spot and been waiting for an opportunity of occupying it.

In writing of dry fly fishing, the expression "good water" has frequently been used, and it may be well to give some idea of what the expression means in the mind of the writer. Good water must be neither over-stocked nor over-fished, and must be water which is naturally capable of holding and fattening trout up to at least three pounds in weight. In the smaller parts of chalk streams, near the source, there is generally water which holds quantities of trout, and where a very large total weight may be killed with a dry fly in a day, but the fish in these places are as a rule satisfactory neither in size nor condition. In some cases perhaps this is so because the water is not fished enough, but in others it is simply because the water itself is more suited to produce quantity than quality of trout. An angler who wishes to enjoy the real excitement of dry fly fishing should try to get water where the trout average at least a pound and a half in weight. In such water two pounders will be fairly common and three pounders not unknown. Where trout average two pounds in weight the fishing may be better still, but I am doubtful of the advantage of having a heavier average weight than two pounds, if the angler has to rely upon one stretch of water only for his season's sport. Where there is no May-fly the trout up to three pounds in weight may be expected to rise more or less all through the summer. Trout above that weight are, taking the season all through, bad rising fish, and the angler has to rely for his sport either upon the May-fly or upon late evening fishing.

An ideal piece of water would be one with broad shallows here and there, but with plenty of deep stretches, not stagnant, but with a good current all down them; its breadth in the deeper parts should be about as much as can be cast across by a single-handed rod, and considerably more on the shallows where wading is possible, and it should be fairly well fished, to prevent it from becoming over-stocked. On such water in a pure chalk stream if there is no May-fly, it should be possible, all through May, June, and July, to have good days with trout averaging nearly two pounds and in the finest condition, and this may be done without relying upon the evening rise. It is not meant by this that every day in May and June, and still less in July, will be a good one, but that there will be several days in May and June, and some days in July, when a good basket can be made before the evening. It will have to be done with small flies and fine gut, and the angler, who lands in this way from five to ten trout, averaging two pounds apiece, on a fine summer's day, need wish for no more delicate and exciting sport in trout fishing. One often reads of days with many three, four, and even five pounders on parts of the Test or Kennet, but I gather that these splendid baskets are made with the May-fly, or with a large fly late in the evening, and that the waters in which such things are possible do not give good fishing in the day-time after the middle of June.

In these days of artificial rearing and careful preservation, there is always a danger even on club waters of over-stocking. I doubt whether there is much risk of this being done by the most lavish distribution of fry, but I am sure it is easily done by turning in too large quantities of yearlings or two-year-old fish, and I have known or heard of instances where the average weight and condition of the trout has been injured in this way, and the sport has suffered in consequence. Any given stretch of river, well preserved and free from pike and coarse fish, can be made to keep alive a much larger total weight of trout than it can fatten; and now that good dry fly water is so carefully looked after, there is a tendency to try to increase both the number and total weight of trout that can be taken in each season from each piece of water. It is easy to do this at the expense of the condition of the fish, and so to ruin the sport for the time being.

The condition of trout varies in different seasons.

One cannot expect the average condition of trout of two pounds and upwards to be first-rate before May, and all through the season some fish will be landed which are not first-rate, but the proportion of these seems to me to vary in different years. In some years the trout seem to thrive better than in others. I am not thinking now of whether they are forward or backward in condition early in the season, but of the average excellence of condition which is reached by the middle of June, after which trout cannot be expected to improve. In May 1887 I noticed that the average condition of the trout landed during the month was exceptionally fine. After that year it seemed to me that, though some fish were as good as the best in 1887, there was not the same universal excellence, and in some seasons there was a real deficiency of condition,[1] though the number of the trout in this particular piece of water did not increase. Now in 1887 there was a very good supply of water in Hampshire chalk streams at the beginning of the season: it fell off greatly towards the end of the summer, and in no subsequent season have we started in May with as good a head of water as in 1887. So, at least, it seemed to me, and I was inclined to think that the condition of the fish was affected by the flow of water: that they throve better, were more active, and had better appetites in a good flow of fresh water. But the year 1898 entirely upset this theory, for in that season in May and June the average condition of the trout in the same water

---

[1] It was in such a season of poor condition that a water-keeper, telling me of the long dark thin trout that were so unduly numerous, described them to me as "completely emancipated."

was again exceptionally fine, though the head of water in the river was exceptionally low. The first suggestion of course will be that the abnormally mild winter of 1897-8 accounted for this, but the winter which preceded May 1887 was not very mild, and other observations have not given me any support for the theory that a mild winter ensures good condition in chalk stream trout.

CHAPTER IV

WINCHESTER

MANY things are taught at public schools, but Winchester is probably the only school at which the most scientific and highly developed form of angling can be learnt. The art was not taught at Winchester in my time, but there were opportunities for learning it, which a few of us did not neglect. Some energy was required to seize these opportunities, for though fishing was not discouraged, no special facilities were given for it; the hours both for work and for games were arranged without any consideration for the time of the rise, and this fact alone made our Winchester fishing different from any other. For the perfect enjoyment of sport the hours of daylight should be all our own. "You cannot compel fish," as an old Scotch keeper used to say when salmon fishing, and an angler needs to have such freedom that, if need be, he can wait for hours upon the will of the fish, and be ready to take advantage of their mood at any moment. This freedom to fit one's own time to suit the changes of sport is essential to the very fullest enjoyment of a day's angling. Every angler should take some pride in being able to satisfy the often prolonged demands made upon his patience, but to appreciate this exercise of patience he ought to feel that there is no reason for hurry, and if he has only one hour

to spend by the river, this is just what he does not feel.
At school the hours are rigid: it cannot be otherwise,
and so far from having any complaint to make, I hope
to show that we were at Winchester more fortunate in
our opportunities for fishing than might, all things
considered, have been expected. I will not say that we
always thought so at the time. The mature judgment
of retrospect is perhaps not the same as the opinions
which were expressed under the impulse of youth and
ardour and the pressure of the moment.

There must have been about a fortnight of the trout
fishing season left when I first went to Winchester in
September 1876, but I was not then in a position to take
advantage of it. Most boys probably look forward to
the first days at a public school with alarm and awe. It
certainly was so with me, and I remember very well
discussing this feeling with a contemporary at a pre-
paratory school. He and I had both reached that
position of comparative ease and security which can be
attained by older boys even at private schools, and we
agreed that we looked forward with dread to exchanging
it for the plunge into the unknown which entrance into
a public school appeared to us to be. Nothing stands
out more clearly in the memories of boyhood than the
first days at a first school, and after them the first days
at a public school. One is bewildered by novelty and
apprehension, and it is not only the outward incidents,
but one's own inner self and its sensitiveness that are
clearly remembered. In looking back to Oxford and
other first experiences of later days, it is but a dim and
blurred outline of feelings that I can recall, but very clear

and distinct are the outlines of a very real self, moving among unfamiliar surroundings, in the first two or three weeks at Winchester. In these weeks I did not even think of fishing; everything about me was so strange; but there were not really any hardships, and as the sense of strangeness wore away, as knowledge came of what might and what might not be done without offending against customs and unwritten laws of opinion, I soon began to rejoice in the comparative freedom of a larger world, in the greater scope of work and games, in the anticipation of all that was before me. I made many plans during the winter for the opening of the next fishing season. The trout could be watched in the Itchen much more easily than in northern streams; they were there before our eyes. On mild autumn days we could watch them feeding, and numbers of them were larger than any I had ever hooked or even seen in the burns of my north country home. Warnings were given abundantly that these trout were not to be caught easily, that with few exceptions no one at school ever had caught any: the traditions were of general failure to which there had been one or two remarkable exceptions, but even in naming these, hints were not wanting that it was very unlikely that any one would succeed again. Nevertheless the trout were there plain to be seen, taking flies, and nothing but experience could have destroyed my hopes or confidence. So on the opening day of the season, at the beginning of March, I hurried as soon as possible into the water meadows. Surely no one ever fished the Itchen with greater anticipation and with less chance of success. I must have been a strange uncomfortable figure, in a large white straw hat, a black coat, trousers and thin ungreased boots, splashing in the meadow (which was under water at the time), and stumbling in haste into the unfamiliar maze of runnels and water cuts. None of these drawbacks were fatal to success. The real obstacle was that I knew nothing, and had heard nothing of the dry fly, and was setting to work with a whippy double-handed rod of some thirteen feet in length, and three flies, probably a March-brown, a coch-y-bondhu and a Greenwell's glory, which I generally used in those days. I remember making straight for a particular spot, which I had often marked in winter as a likely-looking place; it was one where the current flowed away from me under the farther bank and made a ripple. There was no thought of looking for a rise, but the water was fished steadily. No trout showed a sign of paying any attention to my flies, and at the end of the allotted hour I left the river, wet and unsuccessful, but keen and reluctant to leave off. The same thing happened day after day, nothing occurred to break the monotony of failure, and my friends ceased even to ask whether I had caught anything: but it was at any rate a drawn battle, for I had no more thought of leaving off fishing than the trout had of taking my March-browns and other wet flies. At last one day at the very bottom of the water a trout did take my fly at the end of a long line down stream, but it was a tiny thing, hopelessly under the limit of size for the Itchen, one which might have been counted among northern dozens, but could not be brought home alone. During those early days of the season hardly any other anglers were out, and I saw nothing hooked; but as time went on, one or two local anglers, who understood the Winchester trout, began to fish, and by watching them and asking a few questions I came to understand their method. Some flies were then bought from Hammond, who was in those days the great authority upon the Itchen; they were not tied with a divided wing, as is the rule now, but it was possible to make them float, especially the hare's ears, and it was with one of Hammond's flies that I had my first success. This was a long time in coming, for it was not till June that I caught a trout of reasonable size, and that was the only one I caught during my first season. I can see the place and the rise of that trout now, and recall the anxiety and excitement after it was hooked! It was indeed a morning never to be forgotten: all the deferred hope, all the keenness of many weeks, found satisfaction and reward in a moment, the great gulf between failure and success was passed, and I stood on the right side. I had seen now how the thing could happen, and I was sure it would happen again. The trout weighed a little over a pound, and was hooked with a red quill gnat. It was carried home proudly by hand, for I had no landing net in those days; and though there was no more success for me that season, it was henceforth possible to give a willing answer to the question whether I *ever* had caught anything.

A small annual payment gave us the right to fish in about half a mile of the river on the part known as "Old Barge," and the Winchester trout here had ways of their own, the result no doubt of special education. Day

tickets, as well as season tickets, were issued for this
piece of water, and I have seen as many as eleven rods
fishing it at once, the average number of rods in the best
of the season being probably four or five a day. The
effect upon the trout was curious but logical. They
had become very difficult to catch, or else none would
have survived; there were plenty of them, and it was only
partly true to call them shy. As a matter of fact, it was
not nearly so hard to approach them as it is on many
waters much less fished; nor did they take offence very
readily at clumsy casts. It was possible to go on
casting for hours over rising trout without putting them
down, but it would be a mistake to infer that they were
indifferent to bad fishing. I suppose habit had made
them patient of many faults in angling, which would
have been resented at once by fish of less experience.
The presence of a figure on the bank, the coming and
going of the gut and of an artificial fly, became to most
of these trout incidents inseparable from their feeding
time. These things must have seemed to them attendant
on every natural rise of fly, features not altogether
welcome possibly, but on pain of complete starvation
not to be treated with indiscriminating fear. So the
trout rose; they rose freely, and to some extent imper-
turbably, but they discriminated. To the end I never
was quite sure on what success depended most on this
wonderful piece of water. Fine gut and a perfectly
floated fly and exact casting must have been of use here
as everywhere, but these alone were not enough. A
Winchester trout might disregard them all, and there
was no magic attraction for it in the first cast; on the

contrary, I came to look upon it as an exception, if a trout rose at my fly before this had been often floated over it.

Perseverance and continuous rapid work seemed to have most effect. There was one man who understood those fish better than any one else, and who caught far more; he fished nearly every day, and from watching him long and often I became aware of certain peculiarities in his style. Of course he knew the water very well and generally managed to be at a very good place when the rise began, and once there his plan was to stick to his fish and to cast quickly. He dried his fly harder and more rapidly than any one I ever saw, and brought it floating over the fish oftener in a given space of time. His rod and line used to make a very busy sound in the air, as he dried his fly. It was not pretty fishing to watch, but when he made a cast, the line went out straight and accurate, and he once to my knowledge landed in one day from this much-fished part of the river seven brace of trout, all above the limit of size. We used to find him fishing when we came out, and to leave him fishing when we had to go in, but his plan was always the same, to move very little, to watch the river closely when fish were not rising, to cast quickly and incessantly while the rise lasted, and to change from one fish to another, rather than from place to place, all day. He was also a very silent angler, as if his business was solely with the trout, and what he was, besides being the best resident fisherman at Winchester, remained unknown to me. I was so struck by his success in fishing that it never occurred to me to ask about anything else.

One or two of the men who fished this portion of "Old Barge" occasionally, were anglers of renown. There was, for instance, the late Mr. Francis Francis, at that time probably the best known of all authorities on angling; my recollection of his fishing on the Itchen is that he used a double-handed rod, and threw a small fly therewith more accurately than it seemed easy to do with so large an instrument. Sometimes too, but not often, we saw on "Old Barge" the greatest angler I have ever met. One could not say which was the more instructive, to watch his fishing or to listen to his talk; no one had more information to give, no one was more generous in giving it; his knowledge seemed the result not only of observation and experience, but of some peculiar insight into the ways of trout. In the management of rod and tackle he displayed not only skill but genius. Such at any rate is my recollection of what I heard and saw in days long ago, and I gather from many tributes, which have appeared in print since then, that the genius of the late Mr. Marryat was widely recognized, most highly estimated, and most willingly deferred to by those who knew him best.

To enable our school fishing at Winchester to be understood, it is necessary to give some account of hours, for the management of time was most important. As a rule school arrangements did not set us free till twelve o'clock, and my object of course was to be by the water and fishing as soon as possible afterwards. My house—fortunate in all other respects—was unfortunate in being the farthest but one from the river. To have gone there and back after school was over would have been to lose at least ten minutes. This clearly could not be endured; nor must more precious time be lost in putting together a rod. It was necessary to make arrangements by which one could rush from school at twelve o'clock without a moment's delay, with a rod and tackle ready for immediate use, and with things of some kind on one's feet and legs, which, even when the water was "out," would with ordinary care keep a dry inside in the water meadows. Wet feet may be wholesome enough under proper conditions, but even at the age of fourteen it is not good to eat dinner and spend several sedentary hours in wet boots and socks on every afternoon. By various expedients, all these difficulties were satisfactorily overcome, and if nothing untoward happened "up to books" to delay one, and if "dons" were punctual in getting work over, it was possible by running to begin fishing at about five minutes past twelve. Here let me explain how fortunate this was for us,—and by "us" is meant those few of us who cared for fishing, the rest being unconscious of the special good fortune of having this hour from twelve to one o'clock free. It is, on the whole, the most likely hour in which to find trout rising. In cold weather it is often too early; in warm weather it is sometimes too late, but in the best of the fly fishing season, and indeed in any month of the season, on water where there is no Mayfly, it is often the best hour of the rise in the day—using the word "day" as distinct from "evening." If I were forced to choose one hour, and only one, in which to fish daily throughout the season, it would be this hour from twelve to one o'clock. Soon after one o'clock we had to leave the water to go up to house for dinner. It was a compulsory meal for which one might be rather —but not very—late without notice being taken, and the adjustment of this point in one's mind, when fish were rising, was a very distressing business. There are ways my feet have often trod, but in which I have seldom gone at a walking pace; they are those which are the shortest from different parts of the river to the house in which I once was, and many many times have I sped along them, sometimes full of the joy of success, sometimes in exasperation and despair, but nearly always rather late, a rod at full length trembling and shaking in the air as I ran. The best method of making a good use of this hour on "Old Barge" was to choose quickly an unoccupied place where fish were rising, and to stick to it. There would, as a rule, be no success at first, and the trout would go on feeding, apparently with a fixed determination to pay no attention to an artificial fly, but every now and then one of them after much casting would lose its head or make a mistake and be hooked. To land one fish not below the limit of size was satisfactory; a brace was a real success. The result of the best hour which I ever had was two brace and a half, but that was very exceptional. It happened at the end of May, on a day when the water was made rough by a strong wind up stream, and when there was a great rise of full-sized duns, which the trout were taking greedily. On whole school days it was impossible to get a full hour's fishing in the afternoon, and though there was more time on half-holidays, it was very seldom that there was a rise at that time. In the same meadow as this part of "Old Barge," there was another stream, known to the outside world as the mill pond. It was a very dull bit of water with hardly any current, and though it held larger trout than the main river, they did not rise till comparatively late in the season, and then generally in the evening only. These trout were in their habits altogether different from those in "Old Barge." It once happened to me to have a great triumph and land one of them, which weighed three pounds and a quarter. This fish took a grey quill gnat at about five o'clock one afternoon, but as a rule, all we could do on the mill pond was to see occasionally the first signs of the beginning of the evening rise. In summer we could fish early in the evening, but we had to be indoors punctually at eight o'clock, and this was just too soon in June and July to let us have much chance, either in "Old Barge" or the mill pond, though we saw other and freer anglers coming to the water as we left it. There was more discipline to be learnt in this way than in any other at school. To have a passion for fishing, to spend an hour by the river evening after evening watching intently for a rising trout, and invariably to tear oneself away just as the rise began, was a curious experience. There were other parts of the Itchen, where we used to fish—on "New Barge" along the old towing path above Shawford, and from one side under the old elm trees at St. Cross, but these places were farther away, and we generally went there on free afternoons, and then only when, after finding no trout rising in "Old Barge," we roamed about in the vain hope that they might be rising somewhere else.

These Winchester trout taught us the necessity of using fine gut and small flies, and of floating the fly accurately over a rising fish; but they did more than that, they taught us to expect success only as the result of patience and hard work. This was a valuable lesson, which made the fishing in other waters seem easy by comparison. A day on private water, where a feeding trout might reasonably be expected to rise to the first accurate cast, was a glorious delight; something to be thought about for days beforehand and remembered long afterwards. In fly fishing, except on very rare days, or on waters which are over-stocked and little fished, hard work is needed to make a good basket; and to have been used to work hard and to expect little is the best of training. The record of trout above the limit of size (three-quarters of a pound) caught by me on the water described at Winchester, was in 1877 one trout, in 1878 thirteen trout, in 1879 thirty-two trout, in 1880 seventy-six trout, figures which show how severe the training was at first, and how my dry fly education progressed under it.

It would not be suitable for me to attempt to tell here the full tale of my gratitude to Winchester, for to do this would lead me into many reminiscences which have nothing to do with angling. It will be enough to say that the memory of those days is altogether happy, and that the Itchen and its trout played a part in the happiness of them.

CHAPTER V

TROUT FISHING WITH WET FLY

THE enthusiasm which was the result of dry fly fishing led at one time, among those who were fortunate enough to be able to enjoy it, to a tendency to disparage the older art of using the wet fly. A comparison of the two methods is always interesting, but it must never be forgotten that it is not necessary, nor even appropriate, to exalt the one at the expense of the other. It is true that there are rivers on which the two methods overlap, and where each can be used, but even in such places it will be found that the weather, the season, or the character of the water decides from time to time in favour of one method or the other. It is the habit nowadays for nations to divide maps into what they call spheres of influence; a division which sometimes accords with geographical and natural conditions, and at other times is arbitrary. Something of the same kind is possible between the wet fly and the dry fly, but with this advantage as applied to angling, that the division of spheres of influence is not arbitrary, but prescribed by natural conditions, and likely to be maintained by them. Roughly it may be said that the dry fly method possesses the South of England, while the wet fly is superior in the West and North of England, and in Scotland. In the Midlands and in part of Yorkshire there is a disputed

territory where both are used, and where there may be a
real competition between them.

In late years the literature of wet fly fishing has not
kept pace with that of the dry fly.   There is nothing
known to me in angling literature which for scientific
information compares with the books of Mr. Halford
and some other authors on dry fly fishing, but that is
partly because no such uninterrupted and accurate study
of the life of a river is possible in typical wet fly streams.
In the clear water of a gentle chalk stream the habits
both of the trout and of the flies on which they feed can
be studied almost as in an aquarium: not only can more
be seen, but observation can be more constant; no floods
change the conditions of the river and disturb the fish,
while the constant and abundant supply of food has
produced a greater tendency to regular habits on the
part of the trout.   There is nothing in this to detract in
any way from the merit of the authors referred to, but it
does to some extent account for the pre-eminence of
scientific research and knowledge in the books devoted
specially to dry fly rivers.

When, however, we come to discuss the skill required
for one method or the other, comparison is not so easy.
Some dry fly anglers may have spoken of wet fly fishing
as a "chuck and chance it" style, by which small fish
are caught easily in coloured water on coarse tackle.
Some wet fly anglers, on the other hand, may have
expressed a belief that all the talk about dry flies is
superfluous, and that large well-fed trout in clear and
smooth water can be caught by the methods, skilfully
applied, which are successful in north country rivers.

If there be any angler on either side, who still holds such opinions, he can but be advised to put them to the test in practice, and so bring himself to a more just frame of mind.

My own fishing was first learnt among northern trout with a wet fly, but from early years it happened to me to spend all the best of the fly fishing season, year by year, upon chalk streams, till the use of the dry fly became much more familiar to me than that of the wet. I have known and tried enough of the wet fly to be sure that the use of it has very narrow limits in a pure chalk stream well fished, where the season does not begin till May; and also to discover that the experience of dry fly fishing has not been gained without sacrificing something of the knowledge and skill which might have been acquired in the other, had there been equal opportunity. Any one who can catch a Winchester trout should be able to use wet flies with some effect in rivers proper for them, but his basket will not as a rule be so heavy as that of the expert, who has made a special study of the use of wet flies. It is easier to lay down rules for catching chalk stream trout than for catching those of north and west country rivers; neither the flies nor the fish in the latter can be so constantly and clearly watched, and it is not possible to describe so accurately the motion of the one nor the actions of the other, and therefore to say with so much certainty what should be done. In dry fly fishing there is an ideal way of presenting the fly to a fish, and the angler knows when he has succeeded in doing this: in wet fly fishing this process, from the moment the flies alight upon the water, is out of sight, and even the rise itself is often unseen. This is an instance in which the pleasure of the two methods differs. In wet fly fishing the rise or the coming of a fish is more unexpected. Surprise is a perpetual element of the day's work. The angler must be ready to strike at any moment, and it is in this constant readiness to strike quickly that, other things being equal, the great difficulty of this particular method of angling seems to lie. Time after time the rise of a quick, active, north country trout comes upon me like an emergency for which I am unprepared. I fail in the incessant watchfulness of hand and eye that are required, not as in dry fly fishing at an *anticipated* moment, but at all moments, when the unseen flies are in the water. A double watchfulness is needed. The hand must be ready to receive the message from the eye, but must not wait for it, and the least touch under water needs even quicker action than a visible rise. We fish both by sight and by feeling, and many a day there is at the end of which the number of fish in the basket bears a very small proportion to the number of those which have been touched, and which might have been hooked and landed by greater promptness in striking. My own belief is, that in wet fly fishing for trout the more quickly the strike can be made the better, and that nothing but constant practice can give a high degree of efficiency in this respect.

It follows from what has been said that every inch of water should be fished with as straight a line as possible; in still water this is not difficult; in fishing across and down stream it is easy, except in rough broken water, or where the stream is uneven, in which cases a line, which was cast straight, may do all sorts of curious things in the water, and the flies turn out to be in unexpected places; in fishing up stream great care is always needed to prevent the line becoming slack. Here is another difficulty, for assuming that a fairly skilful dry fly angler can throw his wet flies lightly and accurately with a straight line, the management of the line in the water will still be unfamiliar to him. The art of keeping in touch with his flies in rough water is not learnt by the angler on chalk streams. In wet fly fishing, if the line becomes slack, the flies will sink deeper in the water. There is then less chance of seeing the rise of the fish, and the probability is that any trout, which takes the fly, will not be hooked or even felt when the line is slack. At the end of a day's fishing we know of the fish that have been touched or risen, but who can say how many trout have taken the fly and rejected it, unfelt and unseen? Here therefore is another piece of skill required besides that of striking quickly, namely, that of keeping in constant touch with the fly without interfering with its motion in the stream. This is essential to success, but not easy to attain. In still water no doubt a motion must be given to the flies by movement of the hand, but except in still water and in very slow streams it is probably better to let the flies float down and sweep round with such movement as the stream may give them. So much for two respects in which a wet fly angler must be especially skilful to be very successful. He can only acquire this skill by long experience, and my own opinion is, that he can only maintain it by constant practice.

"There are scents in the air and sounds of birds' songs"

(*see* **p.** 96)

To this must be added, among other qualities, a knowledge of the habits of trout living in strong and rocky rivers with streams and pools and shallows. The biggest trout live in deep water, but it is not there that they will be caught with fly in the best of the fly fishing season. In a good day in April or May, trout, which are well on the feed, move up to the shallower broken water near the head of a pool, or to the wide rippling shallows, and it is in water knee deep, or even less, that not only more trout but the best trout will be caught.

Let us take an April day on some northern river. It is a day's fishing that is before us, and the first thought in the morning has been "what sort of a day is it?" Probably that is the first thought of every one who lives out of a town and cares about the country. It is always some sort of a day in the country, not always the sort that has been expected or desired, but one to be looked at, studied, recognized and made the most of in an appropriate spirit. Now and then, but very rarely, there comes a day which is fit for nothing but to sit in the library with one's back to the window. I am sure I have known one or two such days, but I cannot describe one of them. Directly one begins to think of any past day, some feature of weather or light or sky is recalled, which seems to prove that the day had some interest, if only by contrast. The least interesting day is perhaps one with a dull unbroken sky, a very cold but not very strong east wind, the thermometer ranging only from about 32° to 35° in the twenty-four hours, and with neither sun, nor rain, nor snow, nor hail, nor frost, nor indeed anything violent or remarkable. As for great gales and storms there is a fearful joy and excitement about them not to be missed in the country, and rain is delightful.   But the day that I am remembering now is a fine April day—one of the very best.   April is not a warm month, but it has some warm days, and if an angler, who cannot fish all through the month, happens to choose these days for fishing, he ought to count himself a fortunate man.   Such days may come at any time of the month, in the beginning, middle, or end, but in the north, at any rate before quite the end of April, trees will still be brown and bare.   That does not matter.   There will be a spirit in the air, an appeal, a promise, a prophecy, to make a man's heart leap up within him.   There is a feeling of rising sap and reviving life.   It is as if by some great effort of sym-pathy, a new sense had been discovered within us, such as has been imagined for fairies.

> Fairy ears a-listening,
> Hear the buds sprout in the spring,
> And for music to their dance
> Hear the hedgerows wake from trance;
> Sap that trembles into buds,
> Sending little rhythmic floods
> Of fairy sound in fairy ears.
> Thus all beauty that appears
> Has birth as sound to finer sense
> And lighter clad intelligence.

This sense alone would be enough, but there are out-ward and visible signs too.   Green is rising from the earth, and in some places is as high as the tops of shrubs. There are scents in the air and sounds of birds' songs; not the delicate songs of summer warblers, at any rate not in any quantity, but the more robust songs of birds

which have spent the winter in the British Islands, and
know the difference between the winter and the spring.
On such a day in early April these birds will sing as
if this were the day for which they had longed and
waited, as if the highest bliss had come.   Though some
of our feeling about the conscious enjoyment of birds
and other forms of life may be mere fancy, it is
altogether true that there is an ecstasy about the first
warm days of spring which cannot be resisted, and we
cannot tell how much comes from within and how
much from without us.   There is a spirit stirring,
abroad.   We know that we share it, and that it is not
ours alone.   This is what may be felt on the way to the
river, knowing that the day is all before us and that all
the day is ours.   Time was when, eager to begin to fish,
I used to hurry this part of the day, but that was a
wasteful and irreverent habit.   Fishing is to be enjoyed,
but it will not be enjoyed any the more by hurrying past
what Nature has to give us on the way.   There is no
need to hurry, for if the start is made in proper time, the
rise will not have begun before the water is reached.
When the angler reaches the bank the first thing to be
noted is the height and colour of the river, two things
which are taken for granted on chalk streams, but which
vary very greatly on northern rivers, and make a great
difference not only to the result, but to the method
of fishing.

In April the water will probably be low rather than
high, for February, March, and April are on the average
the driest months of the year.   On the other hand, the
autumn and winter rains should have filled the springs

and prevented the river from being as low and as clear yet as it may become in midsummer, though the water should be more free from and less sullied by the small particles of vegetation, which come from the stones and banks and pools in warmer weather later on. A fish may be seen to rise now and then, but it will be nearer the middle of the day before the rise becomes fast and lively, and what first attracts attention are likely bits of water. Some corner or bit of stream will catch the eye, and stir a keenness which makes one impatient of preliminary things that have to be done. It is a right and happy thing to linger over a walk or drive to the river on such a morning; but be the weather what it may, there is no added pleasure to be gained by spending time over putting on waders. An angler cannot even take pride in the way he does this as he may in the care with which he tests his tackle and ties his knots. When all is ready I like to stand either in the water or on a level with it. Besides the increased risk of being seen by the fish it always seems to me in trout fishing that the work is not so well done if the angler is standing much above the water, and that he casts better, fishes better, and strikes better when more nearly on a level. It is of course possible to cast a longer line from a height, but it is not possible to fish so well with a very long line as with one of moderate length.

And now perhaps for some time not very many trout are hooked. If only a few trout of average size for the river, and in good condition, are landed in the first hour or two, there is no reason to be disappointed; all these are so much to the good: the real rise must not be expected till eleven o'clock or later, and any slackness of sport, at any rate up to twelve o'clock, need not be regarded as prejudicing in the least the prospects of the day.   Presently the signs of life, both of flies and trout, will be evident enough, and then the true test will begin. There are days when the trout will rise everywhere and take badly, but a very short time will show whether this is such a day or not.   If the rise is really a good one, and choice of water can be made without interfering with the sport of any one else, the angler should so have arranged matters that he is now, as the rise is beginning, not far from a really good pool, which has not yet been fished. At such times I prefer a good stream at the head of a long deep pool to any other place.   A heavy basket may be made, especially if there is some ripple, on broad shallow reaches of a good river where trout are plentiful, but there is more chance of an unusually large trout where there is deep water not far away, and there is a separate character of its own about a pool, which is attractive and gives a sort of personality to it.   One such comes often to my memory.   It is a pool in a north country river, just large enough to hold salmon, yet not so broad that the best of it cannot be fished easily with a single-handed rod by wading; one bank is the edge of a grass field, the other is fringed with bushes, and the stream slopes from the field towards the bushes. The rough broken water at the top is fairly shallow, and full of good trout when they are feeding.   There are special places at the edge of the bushes in which to make a point of throwing a fly after the nearer part of the stream has been fished.   Each trout that is hooked fights desperately for the shelter of the bushes, or for the deeper water below, and the angler may work slowly down, rising, hooking and landing fish of all sizes, till he gets into deep and quite smooth water.   On a good day a dozen trout at least, none of them less than a quarter of a pound and one or two weighing one pound each or upwards, may be expected from this piece of water alone.

By two or three o'clock the best of the rise will be over, and during the last hours of the day not very much will be added, but it is always worth while to fish steadily with a wet fly, both before the rise begins and after it is over.   This is another instance of the difference between wet and dry fly fishing.   On a Hampshire chalk stream a day's fishing may mean that the angler has spent a day by the river, but it generally does not mean that he has fished all day: on a wet fly river it should mean both, unless there should be some violent interruption from the weather, or unless the water should rise quickly or be in flood and out of order.

In April I do not fish on into the evening, but leave off about the end of the afternoon: after a good day it is pleasant to sit a little on the bank after all signs of trout have ceased, listening to the sound of the water, and thinking with content of what has passed—leaving till a later hour the anticipation of other days that may be yet to come.

Other days there are indeed in April of a very different kind: bitter days when savage gusts smite upon the water and whirl the line about, and hard showers come pelting down from clouds of fearful blackness, and hands are in pain with cold.   Even then there will probably be some time in the afternoon during which the trout will take, though one may have to fish on for many hours before it comes.   I have seen the rise delayed till nearly four o'clock.   One day I well remember at the end of April, when a basket which after some five hours' fishing at three o'clock was light enough, was heavy and full soon after five o'clock.   The day was cold and the rise was very late in beginning, but when it did begin the trout took greedily.

Early in June a passion for taking small red worms seizes the north country trout: the lower and clearer the water, and the hotter the weather, the better do they take.   This lasts till the end of the first week or rather later in July, and is, so far as I can see, quite inexplicable. There is nothing apparent either in the condition of the water, or in the natural supply of food, to excite this violent appetite at this particular time of the year. There is of course no month in which trout may not be caught with a worm, but it is certain that for these few weeks of the season worm fishing for trout is altogether a different thing from what it is at any other time.   It is an art of which I have had little experience.   It needs special skill in casting the worm up stream, a knowledge of when to strike, and, for great success, a practised rapidity in baiting the hook, when trout are being landed quickly.

After the beginning of July the angler may have many a pleasant day's fly fishing though his basket will not often be heavy.   The natural flies continue to hatch out in July and August, and the trout feed upon them, but in dilettante ways, and in all sorts of water—in deep still water, as well as in streams and pools. The rivers will as a rule be very small and clear, and the fish partly for this reason, and partly because they are now less intent at any given time of the day upon feeding, will be more shy and particular. It becomes desirable to cover a larger extent of water than is at all necessary earlier in the season, fishing one bit of water because the light summer breeze happens to be making a fair ripple on it; another because a fish is seen to rise; and a third because it is broken water with good sheltering stones, among which fish may be lying: but neglecting or passing lightly over many a stretch of water, where at the height of the rise earlier in the season dozens of trout would have been hooked. In fact, at this time of the season one has a roaming day, trying many places and many individual fish, succeeding only now and then, pleased with difficulties that are overcome rather than proud of the total, and half inclined to look upon all success as unexpected. Personally on such days I am apt to spend some of the afternoon very quietly, and to fall to remembering how the river looked in the spring and what happened then. Very small and gentle are the best streams of many north country trout rivers in July and August, and have then but a tinkling sound.

> A noise like of a hidden brook
> In the leafy month of June,
> That to the sleeping woods all night
> Singeth a quiet tune.

And the woods are thick and silent at this time.

In September the trout take better, but their condition

is becoming suspect, the days are shorter and the glory of the trout fishing season does not revive.

A perfect trout fishing river is not very large.   There is fine sport to be had in some great salmon rivers, such as the Tweed, but I would rather fish for trout in a smaller river, where the whole of the water can be covered by wading, and where trout can have the main stream to themselves as well as the shallower sides and eddies.   On the broad part of the Tweed the question will occur as to whether it would not be better to use a boat, and thoughts of salmon continually intrude.   The most famous trout fishing river in Northumberland used to be the Coquet, and any one who is curious as to its reputation and merit will find these set forth in the *Coquet-dale Fishers' Garland*.   In size and character and variety of water the Coquet is a perfect river for trout fishing, but the average size of the fish is small, much smaller nowadays we are told than it used to be, and smaller, it seems to me, than it ought to be.   Why this should be so I cannot tell, nor why this change, if change it be, in the average size of the trout has taken place.   There are plenty of trout, it is the size alone that is complained of, and this is the sort of complaint that is very frequent on north country rivers.   Whether it is really founded upon fact, or whether it is only an impression, I cannot say.   I have seen no actual records of average weight in other years which enable me to make comparisons between them and those of the present day, and we are apt to remember the larger and forget the smaller trout of our youth, just as we so often retain an isolated memory of very hot days in summer, or very cold days and deep snows in winter, and take these to be typical of what the respective seasons used to be in earlier years. Another river of which I often think, though it is about twenty years since I have seen it, is the Dart. Here too the average weight of the trout is small, as it seems to be in all west country rivers, but I did not hear upon the Dart the same complaints of a falling off in size. It must not, however, be supposed that there are not large trout in these rivers. I have seen a yellow trout, which weighed several ounces over two pounds, landed from a clear stream in the Coquet on fine tackle in July, but such things are exceptional; and in my own experience, even half-pound trout in these rivers are not very commonly hooked by fly fishers. Apart from this, the Coquet may be taken as typical of what an angler might wish a north country trout river to be. What then should be the average weight of trout caught with a wet fly? and how much should a good basket weigh? Probably answers to these questions will differ. In my own opinion, any north country river of size corresponding with the Coquet, in which the trout averaged three to the pound, would be first-rate trout water, and as in dry fly fishing ten pounds' weight of trout landed by fly fishing would be a good day; whilst fifteen pounds would be a very good day, and twenty pounds or upwards exceptionally good. It has been my fortune to fish such rivers occasionally, but I am not sure that I have ever attained on a river to fifteen pounds' weight of trout in one day with a wet fly. It will perhaps be interesting to compare this estimate of what may be expected or hoped for in a day's fishing with that given by Stewart in his *Practical Angler*.   Stewart probably knew the rivers of the Tweed district as well as any one, and there was no doubt about either his skill or his success as an angler.   He says, "There are not many days from May to October in which an angler, thoroughly versed in all the mysteries of the craft, should not kill at least twelve pounds' weight of trout in any county in the south of Scotland, not excepting Edinburghshire itself."   In the same volume, in another passage, which refers to worm fishing in July, it is asserted that "he is not worthy of the name of angler who cannot in any day of the month, when the water is clear, kill from fifteen to twenty pounds' weight of trout in any county in the south of Scotland."   It must, however, be added that a note, at the end of the first chapter of the seventh edition of *The Practical Angler*, tells us that before his death Mr. Stewart confessed to a necessity for lowering this estimate, and we are warned to take into account his "ideas and habits as to a day; which a jealous gamekeeper whom he had always utterly beaten described as 'twenty-four hours of creeping and crawling.'"

Much has been written about the proper method of fishing with wet flies, whether it is best to fish up stream or down stream.   It is easier to argue in favour of the up stream method, and if two men of equal ability held briefs one on each side, and argued the case against each other before a jury who were without experience of either method, and therefore presumably impartial, the verdict would probably be given for fishing up stream. But controversy is not always the best method of deciding what is the truth, and in most matters connected with angling, partizanship leads to error, just as certainly as in other affairs. There is no fixed rule to be given in this question of whether to fish up or down. Every angler had better acquire both methods, and be guided by his own experience in the use he makes of them. If, like Mr. Stewart, the great advocate of fishing up stream, he discards the other method altogether, and will not yield even to a rough wind down stream, but prefers to contend with it and maintain his theory in its teeth for hours, by all means let him do so; but it will be better that his persistence and confidence should be the result of experience rather than the result of argument or reading. He will at any rate have the satisfaction of having chosen the more difficult part, for it is generally more difficult to manage wet flies well, when they are cast up stream. It is probably as easy to rise trout in this way, but in rough streams, or even in smooth swift water, it is not so easy to be sure of seeing or feeling the rise at once. The flies sink deeper, the line is not kept so straight, for the stream instead of extending it makes it slack. By great care, and very frequent casting in order to rise most of the trout just after the flies have alighted on the water, it is possible to avoid or to overcome these difficulties to a very great extent, but the result of my own experience leads me to prefer to fish across and down stream, except when the water is very small and clear in the summer. I remember one day in August in the lowlands, when the river was full but had cleared after a flood, and I was fishing a quiet smooth stream which ran deep under one bank and became shallower towards the other. It happened that I was on the deeper side, and by throwing a light long line across and down stream, and letting the flies come round with a gentle motion, many trout were caught, but nearly all of them took the fly quite under water when the line was straight down stream. The most successful plan that day was to let the flies hang in the water for a few moments straight down stream at the end of the cast, moving the point of the rod very gently. Other methods too were tried by me that day, but this was by far the most successful.

When trout are feeding freely on natural flies, the moment when the artificial flies just touch the water is perhaps the most likely in each cast, but trout have curiously different moods when feeding, and there are many days when fish rise in the middle or end of the cast (when the flies are sweeping round under water or hanging in the stream), and appear not to be attracted by frequent and light casting. Sometimes feeding trout are very difficult and peculiar, and seem to be attracted by some special attitude or movement of the flies: it is therefore worth the angler's while to experiment attentively and to store in his memory for future use any suggestive experience.

Variety and independence are great charms of wet fly fishing for trout. There is no need of a gillie or attendant to show the pools as in salmon fishing, and to explain the habits of the fish in each different river. Even on a strange river the angler's own knowledge of the habits of trout in general will enable him to use his flies with effect. Intimate knowledge and long experience of any particular river do give the angler who has them, a considerable advantage, and, other things being equal, should make his basket heavier than that of a stranger, and may well give him also a sense of legitimate and innocent pride.　But there is also a pride, both pleasant and just, in drawing upon a store of general knowledge, and applying it unaided to the trout in water which is new to the angler.　If he is a skilful fisherman, and keeps all thought of beating records away from him, he will not be disappointed with the result.　After many years I still cannot say which is better—to fish a new river for the first time, or to fish on a good day water which has been long known, on which one has the best of reasons for expectation and confidence.　Sometimes it is novelty and the spirit of enterprise, at others it is loyalty to old associations and the attraction of comparative certainty, that decide the balance of pleasure.

Of variety of fish and rivers and pools there is no end in this sort of trout fishing.　There are so many sorts of water, from the swift to the still, from the rough to the smooth, and all degrees between them.　The banks and beds of the rivers may be of rock or stones or shingle or sand or even mud.　The height and the colour of the water vary from time to time.　Even the difference of size in the trout is an attraction; there are rivers, where two-pounders are at least possible, where one or two trout of a pound or more may be expected on any day in the best of the fly fishing season, and yet where trout of a quarter of a pound are no disappointment.　The country in which we fish may be the wildest or the most homely—bare and barren, or woody and fertile. If any special choice had to be made, I would choose a river with steep, woody banks as the most attractive of all for trout fishing; and strong streams in a wild, open country for rougher sport, such as salmon fishing. But all have their charms, and memories of wet fly fishing call up a whole world of varied aspects of beauty. In one element of variety alone have dry fly rivers an undisputed superiority, and that is in weeds. In other things I claim for wet fly fishing a greater variety and diversity of interest, both in country and water. Let any one think of the different water which he has fished in Scotch rivers; sometimes it has been water as colourless and nearly as clear as the Test or Itchen; sometimes water which is brown, but clearing after a flood, with small patches of thin white foam borne down the current. For rich colour a river coming from peat is best, and best of all when it is clearing after a flood, and the shallower parts have a crimson colour in the sun. Good too is "the amber torrent" and "the granite basin," as Clough saw them. We must still long to cast our flies in such places, however much we may have been blessed with opportunities of landing large trout in water meadow rivers on a dry fly. The conclusion of the whole matter is, that no amount of dry fly fishing will altogether compensate for the loss of the other, while no north country rivers can satisfy the longing for Hampshire water meadows in the months of May and June.

CHAPTER VI

SEA TROUT FISHING

ALL through May and June the keenest angler may well be content to stay by a good dry fly river, for he is having there the best and most interesting fishing that this part of the season can give him. But after June is over, good though some days in July may be, I own that a certain feeling of restlessness comes over me. I struggle against it, for it seems a sort of disloyalty to the river and the country which have given so much pleasure, but it will assert itself, just so perhaps the migratory instinct works in the nature of birds, some of which leave their summer homes long before the warm days have come to an end, while there is still abundance of food and everything that they need. As the summer goes on it is felt more and more that the glory of the woods of the south of England is over, that they have subsided into a sombre monotony and silence, which will last till autumn. One feels too that the water meadows are a little too soft, and that the air lacks freshness; and so, without consciously desiring a change, one begins to think of rocks and keener air. The even-flowing chalk stream, with its mills and dams and hatches, the river which is so clear and gentle, so docile and perfectly under control, seems just a little tame, till at last there rises up before one's mind the full-formed images of rough noisy streams and great brown pools clearing after a flood.   One stands in thought beside them, and is impatient to be really there.

It may be easy to provide the change of scene, if that is the only thing desired, but how can this change be combined with the best of fishing from the middle of July through August and into September?   Some salmon rivers may, with the help of lucky floods, give good sport at this time, but the angler cannot get the best of salmon fishing now.   It is only grilse and small salmon that he can expect to get at their best.   The bigger fish, with which it really needs a big rod and strong salmon gut to cope, will not, as a rule, be fresh run or in fine condition as they are in spring.   There is, however, one sort of angling that is at its best, and indeed is only good at all in the months of July, August, and September.   These are the months in which the sea trout run up fresh from the sea, and it is in pursuit of them that the best sport is now to be had.   It is not to large rivers that one generally goes in search of sea trout fishing, and the reason for this is to be found partly in the habits of sea trout, and partly in the arrangements made by mankind with respect to rivers and their rents. Large rivers, to which sea trout have free access, will also have numbers of salmon, and if they are let at all will be let at rents for which the presence of salmon is entirely responsible, and which are far in excess of what is charged or paid for the best sea trout fishing alone. Sea trout in a large salmon river are not of much more account than grouse in a deer forest, and are even looked upon as a nuisance when they are running and take a salmon fly freely, whilst the angler is expecting salmon.

If one lived always upon a large river, and could fish all through the season, it would be better in the latter half of July and beginning of August to take only a small rod and fish especially for sea trout, but at this time of year the salmon and grilse are showing freely in the streams and pools where they lie, and the angler, who may only have a very limited amount of salmon fishing in the year, generally takes the chance of getting some of the salmon which he sees, and disregards the sea trout. It is difficult to fish contentedly for smaller fish and not to try for the bigger, when the latter are constantly showing themselves, and the result is that one sometimes wastes the opportunity of first-rate sport with sea trout in order to have a very indifferent day's salmon fishing. I remember one week in July, when sea trout were running on a first-rate salmon river in Scotland.[1] They rested in numbers in a very long stream and pool where they could easily be reached by wading, but salmon and grilse were there too, and I fished with nothing but salmon flies and salmon gut and a seventeen foot rod. I was continually hooking sea trout of all weights from one pound to three pounds, and of course getting no fun with them on such tackle; if I had used a small rod, and been content to fish the sides of the stream and the stiller parts with sea trout flies, I should have had wonderful sport with sea trout, and probably have hooked an occasional small salmon or grilse also, even though it was impossible to cover the whole water properly with anything but a salmon rod. As it was,

[1] The river was the Lochy; the pool was Mucomir, where the overflow from Loch Lochy joins the Spean; the year was 1888.

my total for five days was four salmon (none of them large) and six grilse, besides a number of fresh run sea trout, which were all wasted as far as sport was concerned. The memory of that week is one of wasted opportunities, which have never recurred. On the other hand, if I were by that pool again and the same conditions were present, I should remember that once in July a friend of mine landed fourteen fresh run salmon and grilse in one day from the stream there, and if I gave myself up to sea trout fishing I might be tormented by the thought that I was missing an opportunity of having such a day as he once had. Such are some of the perplexities of sea trout fishing in large rivers.

Large rivers, however, are not the most suitable for sea trout fishing. The sea trout is not content to stay for days and weeks in running water or strong streams, as the salmon is. What it really likes is to get to deep still water as soon as possible; and small rivers giving easy access to lochs, or having deep still reaches of their own, are the best places for sea trout fishing.

The streams and shorter pools of these rivers give the best sport of all, when the fish are there, but it must be remembered that sea trout pass quickly through the running water, and the best river fishing for sea trout is limited to the particular weeks of the season and the special conditions of the river, in which sea trout run up from the salt water. The season during which these fish run in the greatest numbers is in July and August. During these months they accumulate at the mouths of small rivers and burns, going to and fro in the tidal water waiting for a flood. With each flood or spate, as it is called, quantities of the fish move up the river, and when the water is still high, but falling, the angler has his great opportunity.

Let us suppose that he has been for some days on a good sea trout river towards the end of July, that there has been no rain for some weeks, and that he has wandered about for a few days catching hardly anything, but knowing that fish are showing freely at the mouth of the river and waiting to come up. At last there comes rain. First the dust is laid; then the water begins to show upon the road; and presently little white streams appear on the sides of the hills. Still the rain becomes heavier and continues, and the angler goes out in it late in the evening to watch the river beginning to rise. He listens to the sound of rain upon the roof at night, and with the increasing certainty of a really good spate a sort of corresponding current of excitement rises in him. If the morning is fine, small rivers will be high but will soon be falling, and he goes to a favourite part almost with the certainty of good sport. Wonderful indeed is the delight of standing by a pool which for weeks has been too low, the stream at its head a weak trickle, its deep part smooth and almost stagnant, the end of it shallow, clear, and hopeless, and of seeing it now full of agitation, life, and rich colour. The stream which was so desultory before, now sweeps right down and through the pool, rough and noisy at the top, smooth and quiet in the deep parts, but always a good current; and the whole pool seems full of character. Anything may come in such a pool as this, it may be a small sea trout or one of two, three, or four pounds, or a grilse, or a

small salmon. That is the first charm of this sort of
fishing, after fishing for trout in a chalk stream; there
is such great variety of size. The average weight of sea
trout caught, including the small half-pounders, may be
little over one pound, but there is the chance, sometimes the probability, of hooking something of five or
ten pounds or more, for grilse and small salmon are
always met with in sea trout rivers; and even the sea
trout itself gets to heavy weights, though fish of five
pounds and upwards are not common. While the
river is high and the stream strong the best places are in
the smooth currents at the tail of deep pools and heavy
water, and in gentler rippling streams at the head of
long shallow flats, but the only certain guide to the best
places on each river is experience, and if the angler has
no one to instruct him he must learn by fishing all
places which look as if they might hold fish. If he
works hard he will soon find out good places for himself.
It is especially delightful to have knowledge of the water
of a river and the ways of the fish which come up it,
when this knowledge has been gained by fishing alone.
The angler always believes that he has discovered some
special places, which are better known to himself than to
any one else. This belief is very likely true, but it is
also true of other anglers, for experiences differ, and each
season even on a known river adds something to one's
knowledge of it, partly because the bed of the river and
its banks are altered from time to time by floods.

There is another uncertainty about sea trout besides
the glorious one of size, and that is the uncertainty of
where the fish are. They seem to run very much in

shoals, and one mile of a river may be full of them when there are comparatively few above or below. Whenever there has been a spate which has made the fish move, the angler has to find out where they are, and if he does not get them at once in what he knows to be favourite places, he had better try other parts of the river at some distance. He should always remember, however, that the fish may be in the pools he has already tried and may come to the fly later, and that it is easy to waste a whole day in running about without giving any part of the river a thorough trial. There is a tendency in sea trout fishing to spend time in trying to make sure where the biggest fish are. It is well to be on one's guard against this, and to remain where one meets with the first success, or where fish are seen. When a river is high and coloured the fish do not, as a rule, show themselves much by splashing or jumping, but whenever and wherever sea trout do show themselves in this way, it is an invaluable help to the angler, whose first object is to fish where the fish are, and whose great difficulty often is to be sure that he is doing this. What a contrast this is after a Hampshire chalk stream, where one comes to have an idea of the number and size of the trout in each meadow, and how much it adds to the wildness and hard work of fishing! In sea trout fishing there is no waiting about for the fish to come on the rise, but constant fishing and walking and experiment, and on good days the day does not seem long enough to find out for certain where the best of the fish are.

The sea trout is a wild mysterious creature without a home, and its habits differ as much from those of brown

"The sea trout is a wild mysterious creature without a home"

trout as the habits of wild fowl or woodcocks do from those of partridges. Being such a vagrant it never has the chance of the persistent continuous education in the matter of angling and tackle which some brown trout receive, and its standard in the matter of flies and gut and casting is not so high or refined. On the other hand, its appetite in fresh water is more capricious, it is hardly ever on the lookout for any special flies which can be selected, and the angler has to trust more to the mood of the sea trout and his own knowledge of the river after a spate than to any superior excellence of skill beyond the average, or extra fineness of tackle. When sea trout are in the mood they take as freely as brown trout ever do, but in fresh water they are liable to longer spells of indifference or obstinacy. I think that, as is the case with salmon, sea trout do not enter rivers till they have stored up enough fat to last them, if need be, till they have spawned, but either because they still retain the power of digestion, or because they are more active and alert, more easily interested in what comes before them, they certainly rise to the fly much better than salmon do. One which I caught with a fly in a river after a spate disgorged several of the common black slugs, and it is clear therefore that they some- times bring an appetite with them into fresh water. But for all that, sea trout cannot either expect or need to find a stock of food in clean rocky or stony fresh water, and the angler must be prepared for their often behaving like creatures that are quite independent of feeding.

The rise of a sea trout is generally bold and even

fierce. Sometimes it takes the fly with a silent boil, or even without any sign on the surface if the fly is deeply sunk. The typical rise, however, of a sea trout has some sound about it. There is a quick white splash in the dark water, and (if the line is tight) the fish hooks itself. So violent and rapid sometimes is the sea trout's manner of seizing the fly that it is not safe to use very fine drawn gut, for tackle which may be quite strong enough to play and land a three or four pound fish in open water, cannot always be trusted to stand the jerk of the sudden rush with which even a two pound fish seizes the fly. A sea trout is not in the habit of feeding quietly upon flies floating at ease upon the surface. It may do this occasionally, but it is not used to this method of feeding as brown trout are, and it takes a fly moving under water, as if the fly were a thing trying to escape from it. There are days when almost every fish that rises seems to hook itself without needing effort or attention on the angler's part; and there are other days—generally in bright weather when the water is low—when the fish rise short, because they are shy; they just touch the fly, and on these days I think the angler can do a good deal to improve his sport by striking quickly, by using fine gut, and by fishing delicately with a long line. There are yet other days when sea trout rise boldly and playfully, but fail to touch the fly at all; and indeed "fail" is the wrong word to use, for I think that on these days the fish do not intend to take the fly, and their rises are the results of high spirits and exuberant activity. And so the angler appears to have an excellent chance each time of hooking a fish, when the fish has perhaps never opened its mouth at all. Sometimes a sea trout that has risen and not been touched by the hook will rise again, but they are very uncertain in this respect, and I do not fish over one a second time with the same expectation of another rise, that I feel in the case of a salmon that has risen once and missed the fly. Of course one always feels wronged and aggrieved when a sea trout, which has not been pricked and has no excuse, refuses to give another chance, but there are days when fish after fish rises once, without touching the hook, and yet will not rise a second time. On the whole, however, sea trout, when they do rise, may be said to take hold very well.

It was said just now that sea trout fishing was especially dependent upon the state of the water, and it is true that a falling river after a spate is the great opportunity, but the angler need not despair even when the water is at its lowest, if there have previously been floods to bring fish into the river, and if there are fairly deep pools and long stretches of deep still water. The fish collect in these places when the water is low, and if there is a breeze, which blows fairly up or down the stream and so makes a good ripple, a very good basket may be made. Even when there is no breeze and a bright sun, it is possible to have some sport with the small class of sea trout known as "herling" and by various other names. These smaller fish run later than most of the large ones, and are often met with in shoals. They average only between half a pound and three-quarters of a pound, but they fight with extraordinary activity and strength, and they sometimes rise when no other fish thinks of doing so. I was once by a small sea trout river on one very hot bright day in August. The streams were shrunken and weak, the still places were smooth as glass, and the water, as is the case in bare rocky parts of the Western Islands, was very little tinged with peat and exceptionally clear. The fish were in the river, but there was only depth enough for them in quite still water, and to fish in that seemed hopeless. I sat down and opened my box of flies. Ordinary sea trout flies seemed double their proper size on such a day and by such water. One could not think of trying them, and one shuddered at the thickness of undrawn gut, and yet there was the river, and the day, and the fish, and I was alone and seven miles from the lodge. Something had to be done. So I took out a well-tapered trout cast ending in fine drawn gut, and added about a yard of transparent stout gut to the thick end of it. On the fine end I put a plain black hackle fly of a size suitable for brown trout. A really heavy basket was of course out of the question, and I did not rise any large fish, though there were some to be seen at the bottom of the pools; but by using a small rod and this very fine tackle, I did succeed in getting about ten pounds' weight of the smaller fish, and though the largest was under one pound, I had many a good fight. The conditions made the fishing interesting, there was enough success to keep me at work, and if the result was not very remarkable, it was at any rate enough to give a feeling of having over-come difficulties, and saved what seemed at first a hope-less situation. It was very pretty fishing too, for one could see the gleam of the silver fish, even when they came short or took a fly under water.[1] In similar conditions, but with a little breeze, I have found fresh run fish up to a pound and a half in weight rise freely. Fresh run sea trout are at all times exceedingly tender mouthed, and with small hooks one must expect to lose many of them even with the most careful handling.

Of all fresh water British fish the sea trout fights the best in proportion to its size. Its strength when fresh run is greater than that of a brown trout of the same size, and being, as it often is, a stranger to the pool, or at best only a temporary visitor, it does not so often concentrate its efforts upon getting to some known refuge, but rushes wildly from place to place. The fight of a sea trout is thus stronger than that of a brown trout and, if possible, even more active and full of quick turns. There is no fish with which one has to be so much on one's guard against being surprised, either by sudden rushes or by jumps in the air, and as far as the actual playing of a fish is concerned, for sheer enjoyment and rapidity of sensation, I prefer a good fresh run sea trout of three or four pounds in a river on a single-handed rod and fine tackle to anything else.

For this sort of fishing in a small river, I like to use a rod that is single-handed and yet strong. One not only has more sport with the fish hooked on a rod like this, but one fishes more delicately, and can use finer gut than is safe with a double-handed rod; and finer gut makes a considerable difference in the number of fish hooked, except when the water is very much coloured. With a

---

[1] The day described was in 1898, and the water was the lowest part of the small river Coileader, in the Island of Mull.

small rod an angler, who has nerve and patience, will land even salmon successfully on a casting line tapered to end with the finest undrawn gut, provided always that the water is free from obstructions, such as tree roots and weeds, and that the angler can follow the fish either along the bank or by wading.

Every now and then comes the great event of hooking a grilse or salmon on a sea trout rod and fine tackle, and then there is a long and most interesting contest, to which the angler addresses himself with every nerve strung by excitement. At first his business is to be very modest in asserting himself, and to save his tackle by following the fish as much as he can, rather than by letting out line, which may get drowned in the current. But from the first he selects some favourable piece of water below him, and endeavours to conduct the fish towards it. Often enough, in spite of all he can do, the contest drifts away from the desired place; for the fish may get there too soon and carry the angler past it, in which case he must then select with his eye some other place and make that the object of his movements. The best place of all for the last stage of the fight, when the angler feels that the time has come to contend not only for the safety of his tackle but for victory, is a quiet backwater with a shelving bank of gravel, which is even, and free from very large stones. Any smooth shallow place will do well enough, but a backwater sometimes brings sudden confusion and helplessness upon a tired fish. When a fresh grilse or salmon has been landed on sea trout tackle and a single-handed rod, the angler must have made good use of his resources of quickness, judgment, decision, patience and self-control, and should feel that come what may afterwards the good fortune of that day's angling has been assured.

Hitherto angling for sea trout in rivers only has been discussed in this chapter, but probably more of these fish are caught by anglers in lochs than in rivers. It is a pity that this should have to be so, but, if a loch is accessible, sea trout will not rest till they get to it, and there they are content to remain, till they go up the small streams to spawn. Loch fishing is for obvious reasons not so interesting as river fishing. There is not the variety and individuality of stream and pool and condition of water; whilst in most cases it is necessary to fish from a boat, drifting sideways with the wind, so that the angler is always moving involuntarily towards his own flies, which he is at the same time working towards himself. Most people very much prefer to fish from firm ground, where they can cast when they please, move as they please, and stop where they please to linger over a favourite place.

On some lochs, however, the sea trout lie near the sides, and can be reached either from the bank or by wading. There the angler can be independent, and may have very good sport, though the advantage of covering a large extent of water turns the scale in favour of a double-handed rod. Except on very rough days, fine tackle is important in loch fishing, and as in angling from the bank one cannot make sure of being able to follow the fish, it is necessary, not to have a heavier line, but to have more of it. I once hooked a grilse of nearly five pounds on trout tackle, and a single-handed rod, when I had only thirty yards of line on the reel, and when I was fishing from the bank of a loch on which there was no boat. Twice the grilse ran dangerously near to the limit of the line; twice as a last resource I slacked the line as much as I could, in the hope of making the fish think it was free and cease its efforts, and each time it seemed puzzled, and let me very quietly and cautiously recover some line. Whether a catastrophe was really averted by these tactics I cannot be sure, but they are worth trying in an emergency. That grilse, at any rate, was landed.

In lochs the fish are even more capricious in their moods than they are in rivers. One generally attributes these moods to the weather; there always seems to me to be something in the weather, on any given day, when the fish will not rise, which is the cause of my having no sport; and being of an excessively sanguine temperament —of which I hope never to be cured—I discover that evening some change, actual or impending, in the wind or the sky or the temperature, which I am satisfied will make the next day entirely different. I look forward full of happy expectation. Yet with all this study of weather, I have not been able to arrive at any theory which is satisfactory.

The best day I ever had with sea trout in a river was when the water was not very high, and there was a gloomy gale from the east in August.[1] The best day I

[1] This was on the little river Fleet in Sutherland. The day seemed so propitious that I made but a late start. The number of trout caught was twenty-two; the majority were not large, but several were from two to three pounds in weight, and I had to carry them all. They were caught in about half a mile of water immediately below Rogart Station.

ever had on a loch was bright and hot, and with only a
very slight breeze—not nearly enough in appearance for
fishing. Till midday I had not had one rise, and had
only seen two fish. Then the breeze improved just
enough to make a small ripple, and quantities of daddy-
long-legs came upon the water; the little black loch
trout all under four ounces were very pleased with these
straggling insects, and pursued and took them. I did
not actually see a sea trout take one, but the large fish
began to show by making boils on the surface, and my
belief is that the daddy-long-legs were the cause; and
wherever the sea trout showed, and I could reach them
from the bank, they took my fly.[1]

There is very interesting sea trout fishing to be had in
Shetland, of which I once had some experience. It was
on a property of some 12,000 acres, remote from all
hotels, and so indented by small and large voes that the
actual coast line was about thirty miles, all wild and
rocky. There were innumerable lochs, but the overflow
of most of them fell into the sea over some precipice,
which no fish could ascend, and the sea trout lochs were
practically only two in number. Two burns flowed
from these lochs to the sea, and joined each other about
a mile from their common mouth. Very little was
known about the fish, as far as angling was concerned,
and I found myself—for I was alone in the first days—
with the delightful prospect of exploring the possibilities
of salt and fresh water, remarkable both for extent and
variety. When first I saw the burn it was very low, and

---

[1] This was in the latter part of July 1898, and I was fishing from the
bank or wading on the lower end of Loch Ardglass in the Island of Mull.

the deeper part of it looked like a sulky black ditch. This burn had then so little water that it seemed impossible any fish could have got up the rocky places at the mouth, but even then there were fresh run sea trout up to two pounds' weight in the black peaty holes, and they took a fly well. When a spate came in the last week of August, and in other spates during September, quantities of sea trout and grilse came up this burn, and we always found a number of fresh run fish in its pools willing to rise at all heights of water.

The lochs were less satisfactory. There was no boat upon them, the bottom was of soft peat, and the wading peculiar. After wading a few steps into the water, one's feet sank into the soft bottom, masses of bubbles came up with a wallowing sound, and one had an impression of standing upon a yielding surface, which would collapse suddenly and let one down into an abyss. There was no firm ground in the lochs whatever, but we became used to the alarming feel of the soft peat and to the bubbles, and in time lost our fear, though we observed a certain caution to the end. The most troublesome habit of the lochs was that of becoming quite thick after a night of wind and rain, and even in the rare and short intervals of quiet weather the water in them was always full of floating particles. I think the fish would have risen better in clearer water, but even as it was we found that some fish would take so long as the colour of the lochs remained black; when the colour became brown, fishing in them was hopeless.

The third and most interesting sort of fishing was in the voes in salt water. There was one voe some two miles in length, with two small burns about a quarter of a mile apart at the head of it. It looked a likely place upon the large map, and we walked over to it one Sunday afternoon to see and hear what we could. There were a few crofters near the sea at the place, and we were told by one of them that fish were seen jumping in the voe in September, and that some one was supposed to have fished there once and caught nothing. We thought this hopeful, for where fish are seen in Shetland they may be caught, and one day I walked over to experiment. I seldom spent a more wretched and hopeless morning. There was no sign of a sea trout, and to be wading amongst sea weed, throwing small flies in common salt water with a split cane rod, seemed quite foolish and mad. The burns were only large enough for minnows, and I could see that there was nothing in them. Discomfort was added to hopelessness, for my mackintosh had been forgotten, and some miles of rough peat hags and bogs were between me and the house: the morning had been fine, but about ten o'clock a series of cold, pitiless storms began, which lashed the voe with wind and heavy rain. This would not have been intolerable, if it had not been for the long waders, without which the deeper water of the voe could not be reached; but to stand in heavy rain with waders nearly up to the arm-pits, and without a short mackintosh, is to turn oneself into a receptacle for collecting fresh water. Desolate hills rose immediately behind, and as each storm came frowning up over the top of them, I retired from the water and crouched behind an old boat on the shore till the fury was past. After some hours of flogging the sea, hooking only sea weed, and dodging the storms, there was no spirit left in me. Blank despair overwhelmed me, and I turned to go. My back was to the water, but I had got only a few paces from it when I heard a splash, and looking round, saw where a fish had jumped, the first sign of one seen that day. I went straight to the place and caught a sea trout almost at once, and in the few remaining hours of the day landed sixteen pounds' weight of fish with fly. It may not seem a very heavy basket, but it was something to carry over the moor in addition to heavy waders, and not to be despised as a contrast to the prospect of the morning. I had a delightful reaction from despair to good spirits, and the satisfaction which perhaps a successful prospector or pioneer feels in a new country. The largest fish that day was under three pounds, but I lost one or two good fish in sea weed, and saw some much larger.

We still had much to learn about that voe and the trout there. They moved with the tide, and we had to understand their habits and follow their movements. Sometimes the burns had been in flood, and brought down muddy fresh water which floated on the top of the sea water. A good wind soon carried this out to sea, but if the wind was blowing up instead of down the voe, it dammed back all the burn water at the head, and made fishing impossible. Much time was spent in learning these and other tricks or secrets of the place.

Some of the trout in the sea were brown trout. The largest we caught weighed four pounds and three-quarters, and several were over two pounds. They were perfectly distinct from the sea trout, and had yellow under-sides and some red spots, but their flesh was in colour and flavour that of sea trout. We saw several grilse and small salmon jumping in this voe, and in October they turned quite red without having been in fresh water at all, but we did not succeed in hooking any of them. I suppose that none of the large fish, neither salmon, sea trout, nor brown trout, attempted to enter the little burns till they were quite ready to spawn. They then could have gone only a little way up in a flood, and no doubt returned to the sea immediately after having spawned.

We were told that there were no true salmon in Shetland, but in a large burn we certainly caught many fish from three pounds to six pounds, which were exactly like grilse, and would have been called grilse without hesitation anywhere else. They were quite distinct from the sea trout, though the latter overlapped the grilse in size, and our largest sea trout were heavier than our smallest grilse. Some of the large fish, which were jumping in the voes, were apparently salmon, and perhaps we might have hooked some of them, if we had used some large bait instead of flies, but we were always having some success with flies, expecting still more, and experimenting with flies of different kinds, and so the time passed away. In spite of the forked tail and other distinctions, I cannot say that I always find it quite easy to be sure whether a fish which I have landed is a large grilse or a small salmon: but the difference between sea trout and grilse seems to me clear enough, for the one is unmistakably a trout, and the other is not.[1]

---

[1] The house in Shetland was Lunna, the large burn was the Laxo burn, the voe described was Swining Voe.

Migratory *salmonidæ* are generally divided into three species—*salmo salar*, *salmo eriox*, and *salmo trutta*. Of *salmo eriox*, the bull trout, I have had no experience. It has the reputation of being a powerful fish, but a very bad riser, and in rivers such as the Coquet of being almost useless for angling purposes. As a kelt it takes a fly well enough in the spring. *Salmo trutta*, the salmon trout, is, I believe, the best sporting fresh water fish for its size in the world. There seem to me to be two distinct classes of *salmo trutta*. There is the mature fish, which ranges in weight from one pound up to five pounds as a rule, and may grow exceptionally to much larger weights; and there is a smaller fish, which enters the rivers rather later in vast quantities. This latter ranges in weight from four ounces to any size up to one pound. It goes by various names on different rivers, but is commonly supposed to be the grilse of *salmo trutta*, and both in its appearance and in its rash unwary nature it has all the characteristics of being a young fish, which is mature neither in mind nor body. In most rivers, however, these fish of the smaller class seem to outnumber the mature sea trout of all ages, which is not the case, taking all the season through, as between grilse and salmon.

Sometimes I think that sea trout fishing is the best of all sport. It combines all the wildness of salmon fishing with the independence of trout fishing, and one may have all the excitement of hooking large fish without using a heavy rod and heavy tackle. There is less rule and less formality about it than there is about salmon fishing, and there seems more scope for the individuality of the angler. Perhaps this is partly because the sea trout season comes so directly after a long period of work in the stale air of cities in summer, and coincides with the first burst into freedom and fresh atmosphere. The difference is so great in August, after a few days of exercise in the air of the North, that there come times when the angler, who wanders alone after sea trout down glens and over moors, has a sense of physical energy and strength beyond all his experience in ordinary life. Often after walking a mile or two on the way to the river, at a brisk pace, there comes upon one a feeling of "fitness," of being made of nothing but health and strength so perfect, that life need have no other end but to enjoy them. It is as though till that moment one had breathed with only a part of one's lungs, and as though now for the first time the whole lungs were filling with air. The pure act of breathing at such times seems glorious. People talk of being a child of nature, and moments such as these are the times when it is possible to feel so; to know the full joy of animal life— to desire nothing beyond. There are times when I have stood still for joy of it all, on my way through the wild freedom of a Highland moor, and felt the wind, and looked upon the mountains and water and light and sky, till I felt conscious only of the strength of a mighty current of life, which swept away all consciousness of self, and made me a part of all that I beheld.

CHAPTER VII

SALMON FISHING

SALMON fishing is the greatest of all the sports that can be had in fresh water. I say "fresh" water, for I have had no experience of tarpon fishing, and though the written accounts of it convince me that salmon fishing is a finer sport, I am content to leave any comparison between the two sports to those who know both. I am not sure that we all feel for salmon fishing that intimate affection which we do for some other forms of angling, but the greatness of it as a sport is indisputable, and we admit its supremacy. The attraction of it is found in the largeness of the fish, the size of the rivers, the strength of the stream, and the tremendous uncertainty.

There is exhilaration and excitement and mystery about it, the thought of which hurries us towards any opportunity of angling on a river which is known to hold salmon in any quantity. But we come to be fastidious as we grow older, and though the season of fly fishing for salmon lasts from about the middle of January on some rivers in Scotland to the end of November on the Tweed, we do not look forward to all parts of it with the same eagerness. It is on fresh run spring salmon that the angler of experience comes to set his heart, and for these, on the rivers of Great Britain generally, the months of March and April are the best season. If I had to choose four weeks in the year for salmon fishing, I should take them from the middle of March till the middle of April. It was once my great good fortune to spend a little time in these months for several successive seasons on one of the best spring rivers in Scotland,[1] and since those days I have made comparatively little account of autumn fishing. The glory of salmon fishing is in the spring. In March the supplies of water are still high, from the rain of the autumn or from lately melted snow, which has soaked into the ground. The rivers are kept full, the salmon can ascend them at will, and can be in their favourite places in the streams; and, unless the season be very exceptional, we can rely upon having enough water for angling.

It is a great moment when, for the first time of the season, one stands by the side of a salmon river in early spring. The heart is full with the prospect of a whole season's sport. It is the beginning of a new angling year, and the feel of the rod, the sound of the reel, the perpetual sight of moving water are all with one again after months of longing and absence. Every stream looks as if it must hold a salmon, and as if the salmon must rise, and one begins to cast trembling with excitement and eagerness. Very delightful are the first few minutes, the supply of hope seems inexhaustible, and one bestows it lavishly upon each cast. If the best part of the first pool is reached and passed without a rise, the angler begins to husband his hope a little, but remains

[1] The Helmsdale from 1889 to 1892; at that time it was *par excellence* an early spring river.

still content, reaching forward in thought to the next pool, where he presently begins with fresh eagerness and confidence.

To me there is nothing in all sport equal to the glory of success in salmon fishing, but the supreme moment is undoubtedly the actual hooking of the fish.   However great my expectation and keenness, the feel of the fish when it hooks itself comes upon me with a shock of surprise and delight, and there is a sudden thrill in having to do with the weight and strength of a salmon. A sense of complete achievement and satisfaction is felt merely in the hooking of it.   This satisfaction in hooking a salmon remains undiminished as years go on, but I cannot say the same of the actual playing of the fish.   I remember being a little disappointed even with the first salmon which I played on a salmon rod.   It so happened that I was, when a boy, particularly unfortunate in salmon fishing.   For five years from the time I was fifteen I had a few days' salmon fishing in August or September every year without ever hooking a fish. During all this time I built many castles in the air, and imagined the play of a salmon to be like that of a trout, increased many-fold, not only in strength and endurance, but also in liveness.   Of course it was wrong and unreasonable to expect this combination, and when at last success came, I was struck with what seemed to me a want of quickness in the movements and turns of the salmon. I still feel that want of violent rapidity, and though the play of a fresh run salmon is often very fine, I wish that it was a little less stately.   In some of the more rapid rivers of Norway the speed and violence of the salmon seem to be much greater than they can be in the quieter rivers at home, and some day perhaps I may meet with one of those fish, to land which one has to spend hours and travel miles in the struggle after it is hooked. I have never yet had a fish in play on a salmon rod for more than half an hour, or landed one more than 200 yards from the place where it was hooked.

The art of fly fishing for salmon bears no relation to any other form of angling with a fly. If it is akin to anything, it is to working a minnow rather than a fly, and the salmon angler must get all analogy with trout fishing out of his head. The most essential points are skill in casting and knowledge of the river. In casting the object of the angler is to throw the fly above and beyond where he hopes the fish are lying, in such a manner that it may be brought by the stream moving in a lively and attractive way within sight of the fish, being gradually swept across to the angler's own bank. To do this successfully the angler must cast not only across but down the stream, and the more down stream the cast can be made the slower will be the pace at which the fly crosses the river, the greater will be the chance of the salmon seeing it, the less will be the chance of its seeing the line, and the more easy it will be for the angler to keep in touch with the fly during the whole time it is in the water. This is why it is so important to be able to throw a long line in salmon fishing, even in a comparatively narrow river: it is desirable not only to reach the whole of the likely water, but to cover it at a proper angle. If the cast is made directly across the stream, the line bags in the middle, and for the first half of the cast the fly has the appearance of a dead thing being towed down stream by a visible cord, instead of something alive being jerked by its own motion in the water. Two things especially should the angler bear in mind when actually casting and managing his fly: the first is that the salmon in fresh water has more curiosity than appetite, that it is not waiting for food, nor expecting it to come to it as it lies in the water. The fly must rouse the attention of the fish, and must do it attractively. It should have the appearance of something trying with difficulty to escape from the fish, and so perhaps arouse in it the passion of the chase, even when it has no appetite to be appealed to. This is why I think it is important that the fly should cross the stream slowly, but with a lively motion. The second point is that, as salmon lie either at the bottom of the river or not far from it, the fly should be well sunk in the water. To secure this in heavy water it is best not to jerk the fly violently, but to trust the stream to give the motion to the fly; and to use a long and heavy line. The most successful salmon angler, of whom I have ever had any knowledge, always fished with a big rod and a heavy and long line in the spring. I think his fish nearly always took under water, but he caught more than any one else on that river.

If we could watch salmon more in the water, as we can so often watch trout when feeding, we should learn much that would be of great practical advantage in angling, both in working the fly and in choosing size and pattern of fly for each day. After fishing for a few hours without a rise or a pull we get the impression that the salmon are not to be caught, and are taking no notice of the fly at all, but the latter is probably much less often correct than is supposed. Such opportunities as I have had of observing the behaviour of salmon at rest in the water lead me to think that the fish are continually taking notice of the fly and following it when we do not see them. I was once fishing with a friend on a beat of the Spean in June when the river was very low. We came to the Galleries, one of the best pools, and found it so low and clear that we felt sure that it was not worth fishing, but when standing on a high rock above the pool we saw one good salmon of nearly twenty pounds' weight, and four or five small ones, lying together on a patch of smooth flat stones in the middle of the bed of the river. It was agreed that one of us should go down and fish the pool, while the other remained above to observe what happened. My friend went first, and as soon as the fly reached the fish, one of the smaller ones followed it without breaking the water. Time after time the fly was cast in the same place, and one or other of the smaller fish continually noticed it by some movement, or followed it to the bank, but there was no rise, nor was the fly actually touched. Then I went down and my friend reported from above. I succeeded in moving the big fish; it followed my fly two or three times, but none of the smaller fish made any movement. Then my friend tried again and moved more than one of the smaller fish, but without getting a visible rise from any of them or stirring the big fish. When my turn came again the smaller fish never moved, but the big fish followed the fly right round, and at last made a rise at it with a visible boil at the end of the cast, but without being touched by the hook. That was our nearest approach to hooking a fish, but we had enjoyed half an hour's very exciting sport. It was impossible for the person fishing to see these salmon while casting over them, and had either of us been alone, the angler would never have persevered long enough to get the one visible rise which we did get, and would have asserted afterwards with perfect confidence that not a fish had been stirred. One curious point was, that though we changed patterns and sizes of flies, and interchanged them with each other, I could not move one of the smaller salmon, but only the big one, while my friend at different times moved every one of the smaller fish and never the big one. We had also on this day a very good illustration of the value of knowing a river. We had often fished this pool before, when it was in better order and the fish were not visible, and we now saw that the fish were lying in exactly that part of the pool where we had most often risen or hooked a fish. The reason seemed to be in these particularly comfortable looking flat stones, on which the salmon rested, but till we had once seen this, we had never realized the special virtue of that one spot in the whole pool. An old gillie, who had known a Highland salmon river for very many years, once told me of a similar experience. There was a deep black stretch of the river, about a quarter of a mile long, where the water flowed with a smooth even current between high wooded banks. This part was fished from a boat, and the old gillie told me that for years he had known that in all heights of water there was only one particular bit of some six yards in the whole of it that was worth fishing; but he neither knew nor could guess the reason, till there came an unprecedented drought, and for the first time in his life he saw the bottom of this part of the river. Then going quietly down it all in a boat he saw the salmon lying together at this one place on some stones which were more flat and smooth than the surrounding rock and gravel.

This sort of knowledge must be learnt, in the first place, from those who know; we must in salmon fishing at first profit by the experience of past generations on each river and take it on trust. It would need a lifetime to discover the best places of a river afresh for ourselves. A salmon angler of great experience may make some good guesses at the favourite spots of a strange river, but even he is sure to mistake some useless places for good ones, and to pass lightly over some of the best. Now the most essential thing in salmon fishing is concentration on the best places; it is not enough to be told which are the good streams or pools, and to fish them all with evenly distributed care. The angler should fish all that he is told is good water, but he should concentrate his care and skill and perseverance on the best spots of the good streams and pools. The most successful salmon angler is one who feels expectation—it is more than expectation, it is almost faith, founded on previous experience—stir within him as he approaches certain well-known places. It is as if there was some magnetic influence in the angler's confidence, which predisposed the salmon to take his fly, and an angler who knows that he is fishing a good pool, but does not know exactly where to expect a rise in it, has not so good a chance of rising a fish as the man who has hooked salmon in that pool before, and knows not only that it is a good pool, but what is the best spot in it.

And yet salmon fishing is more lucky than any of the other kinds of angling discussed in this book. Luck does perform the most extraordinary feats on salmon rivers, and plays all sorts of tricks sometimes, but none the less is it true, that the angler who throws the longest line well, and knows the river best, will hook most fish in the season.

I know nothing which raises anticipation to such a pitch as salmon fishing, and nothing which so often wears it down by sheer unrewarded toil. There is much monotony about it; each cast down a long even stream is very much a repetition of the one before it, and when there is no result the angler first loses expectation, and then hope, and falls into a dull mechanical state. In summer and autumn salmon and grilse are often jumping and showing themselves, but in early spring there are no grilse, the fresh run salmon do not jump, and you some- times cast all day without seeing any sign of fish, except kelts, even when there are clean fish in the river. I must admit that, after casting for hours without a rise, great despondency comes upon me, when it is a question of fishing a second time over a long piece of water that has already been tried with one fly without success. How often have I sat on the bank and looked at the unsuccess- ful fly, and wondered whether it was too big or too little, and then at my other flies, feeling that there was no reason why any one of their patterns should succeed

better than the one already tried; till at last I have looked
at the unconscious water and doubted whether there were
any salmon there that day at all!

I have never been very successful in salmon fishing.
Another angler once caught over fifty fresh run salmon
with fly in six consecutive days in March on a river [1] on
which I was fishing at the same time. That is the best
record for the United Kingdom of which I know, for I
should not count any number of autumn salmon or of
salmon caught with minnow as against these. My own
total for those six days was fifteen clean salmon. I was
sharing a rod with a friend, and in consequence only
fished for half of each day, but I felt that under no
circumstances should I have come near to my neighbour's
figures.

I once caught two fresh run spring salmon in one day
which weighed over 50 pounds together. The actual
weights were $29\frac{1}{2}$ pounds and $21\frac{1}{2}$ pounds. The first
one rose to my fly four times before I hooked it. After
the first rise I made a mark in the bank, walked back a
little and fished carefully down to the place again. Each
time that I reached the mark the fish rose, but I had no
idea of its size till, after being played for some time, it
rushed to the other side of the river and splashed and
kicked in shallow water—and a very uncomfortable
moment that was. [2] The second fish took under water
in the middle of the river at the tail of a rapid stream,
and for quite a perceptible number of seconds both the

[1] The Helmsdale in March 1891 or 1892.
[2] The upper part of the lower Torish Pool on the Helmsdale, fishing from
the left bank early in March 1889.

gillie and I thought I had hooked a rock. But when it did move it became lively enough.[1] Those no doubt are no great events compared to the success of others, but if it is a question of competing in records of bad days I think I can do better. I once fished every day for four weeks on a good beat on a good river in the Highlands in September and caught only two salmon. They were both under fifteen pounds, were both red, and one of them never rose at the fly at all, but happened to foul hook itself by jumping on the top of the gut in a swift stream. Another season I fished for ten consecutive days during what should have been the very best fortnight of the spring fishing, on one of the best spring rivers in Scotland.[2] The water was in order the whole time, but I not only never landed one salmon, but never even had a rise. On the last day of all my fly was taken by a fish under water, and I landed a—sea-trout kelt! Finally before the day was over my rod broke in two. It is difficult to believe that it all happened without design on the part of some hidden power, which took delight in watching my long blank days of disappointment, then in mocking me with a sea-trout kelt, and which at last in sheer hatred and malice broke my rod.

I have found the weather very interesting in March in the north of Scotland. More than once the river has been frozen. There was one exceptionally severe frost in March 1891, which for a few days made fishing impossible. In the first days of the frost we used to

---

[1] The upper Torish Pool, fishing from the right bank.
[2] The Helmsdale in early April 1890.

"Then one sees the grouse"

break the ice at the sides of the best pools and push it out in large pieces into the open stream in the middle, which gradually carried it away. By this means we used to get a little clear water in which to fish during the middle of the day, but every night the frost became more and more severe, and at last there was no open water left except just the rough streams at the head of the pools, which after a few yards plunged under a sheet of ice unbroken from bank to bank. I have no accurate record of the shade temperatures of that time. There was a thermometer hanging on the side of the lodge exposed to the sun in the daytime, which registered remarkable extremes. On one night it fell to 5° (27° of frost). The following day was still and cloudless, and with the sun full upon the wall the thermometer rose to 90°. The next night it fell to 3° (29° of frost). I remember in the daytime spreading a mackintosh upon the snow, and lying in the March sun without an over-coat in great comfort, looking at the frozen river. In very severe frosts, when the air is very still and cold, the water freezes on the line, the fly becomes frozen hard and stiff, and the line with its coating of ice becomes too heavy for casting. The smaller rings on the top joint of the rod then become solid blocks of ice, and the line cannot run. You thaw the fly in your mouth, strip the ice off the line and clear the rings, but it all forms again, and little progress is made. In a moderate frost, when the sun is strong and thaws a little snow and ice in the middle of the day, the river will rise a few inches in the afternoon. I remember one March when this happened for several successive days, and in consequence we

invariably hooked one or two salmon at the same hour
in the afternoon.   As long as the frost lasted, this was
the only good hour of the day, but it was a certainty.
The only drawback was that the slight thaw and rise of
water brought down a quantity of small detached pieces
of soft ice, which interfered with the working of the fly,
and were often caught by the hook.

There are other days in March which are typical of
spring, very bright, and caressing one with warm
breezes.   Then one sees the grouse in pairs walking
about tamely, the cock bird with a crimson crown, full
of play and pride, and showing off with various antics;
while the clear air vibrates with the most wonderful of
all the notes of birds, the prolonged spring notes of
curlews, the most healing sound that ever was, full of
rest and joy.

One great charm of the actual fishing for salmon is
found no doubt in casting right out into dark rushing
water; in having to do with the full force of a strong
river instead of with shallows and gentle places in small
streams, as in fly fishing for trout.   Each has its charm,
but the unobtrusive delicacy of trout fishing is out of
place in a salmon river.   Angling for salmon is coarser
work, but it requires skill, and the effort and surroundings are most stimulating.   In spring, too, there
is a great sense of mystery about the water.   Fresh run
salmon do not jump at all, or show themselves much in
the early part of the season.   The angler may see
nothing, and yet hope for everything: the number of
salmon in any part of the river varies continually, and
each day, as the angler watches the river, the water

betrays none of its secrets; they remain hidden till his fly discovers them.

In May, and in dry seasons often in April, salmon angling is apt to be spoilt by want of water, and this difficulty remains till autumn, though each flood ought to bring up fresh fish, and the angler who is always on the spot may have many good days. In July the grilse run in numbers, and favourite streams and pools become alive with jumping fish of all sizes and colours, but except when there is fresh water in the river they take very badly. I have fished on such a river as the Lochy in August till I have been exasperated and made weary by the sight and sound of fish jumping, splashing, making boils, showing heads and tails, and doing every-thing except take my fly. In summer the fresh run fish are generally either small salmon or grilse, but when the water is in order there are plenty of such fish in first-rate condition to be caught. Very good sport may then be enjoyed, especially on a small rod and light tackle, but my experience has been that August and September are very bad rising months on large rivers. October is on the average the wettest month of the year, and in ordinary seasons the rivers become full again, and the salmon that are in them take better, and continue to do so in November, but to me much of the charm has then gone. It is true that on a river, such as the Tweed, fresh run salmon may be landed in November. They are fresh from the sea, but they have neither the liveliness nor the hard condition of spring fish, and in all autumn fishing, the greater number of the fish landed are either red or discoloured. Perhaps I have become unduly fastidious, but I cannot care for autumn fishing with the same eagerness as in past years, and cannot get away from a sense of regret and discontent caused by the appearance of the fish at that season. It is essential to the perfect enjoyment of salmon fishing that the fish which is landed after hard work and a long struggle should be brilliantly white, with all the redness and strength and goodness accumulated by rich feeding in the sea still stored in its flesh.

A Blue Book about salmon was published last year (1898), which contains most interesting but rather depressing information. It has given rise to much controversy, chiefly, I think, because in some comments made upon it the conclusions to be drawn from the book have been stated too absolutely. To say that unspawned salmon never take food in fresh water at once provokes a statement that they take worms and swallow them. We all know this; but the fact that a salmon will often swallow a bunch of worms curling just in front of his nose, or has occasionally been seen taking natural March-brown flies in spring, and been caught with an imitation of them, does not prove that there is no conclusion to be drawn from the very careful scientific investigations described in the Blue Book.

The result of these seems to me to confirm, beyond all possibility of doubt or dispute, a fear which has always haunted me when salmon fishing, and weighed upon my spirits during long days and hours of effort without success. This conclusion is that it is not in the least necessary for salmon to feed in fresh water after coming from the sea, and that we who fish for them are dependent for our success upon their caprice, whim, temper, curiosity, or any chance emotion known to fish, except appetite. In angling for trout we rely with some confidence upon their appetite. If the fish are there we conclude that they will feed at some time, and we expect to succeed when they do. But that upon which we rely in trout fishing is absent in the case of salmon in fresh water. Salmon do not need food then at all, and it has been asserted that the stomach is so changed that they cannot digest much, if anything, and presumably therefore do not hunger.[1] The wonder is that salmon should ever be caught by angling in fresh water at all, and as a matter of fact there is said to be one variety of Pacific salmon which never is caught in this way; but the rule with British salmon is happily less absolute.

Apart from the angler's skill and knowledge of the river, success in salmon angling depends more upon the condition of the water than upon the weather. It is better to fish in the most unlikely weather when the water is in good order, than in the best of weather when the river is rising or " dead low." The most certain time of all in which to get a salmon is when the river begins to rise. If the angler is then at a good stream or pool and the salmon are there, he will probably hook a fish; but this favourable opportunity only lasts for ten or twenty minutes or half an hour. The more quickly the water rises, the shorter will this happy period for angling be, and after it is over there will be no more sport as long as the water continues to rise. The serious business of a salmon in fresh water is to work his

[1] I believe that later investigations have qualified this statement.

way up stream. He does this when the water is rising, and when he is fairly engaged in doing it he will not look at playthings. It must also be borne in mind that fish do not as a rule take well when they are expecting a flood, and it follows that a day on which the river rises is likely to be a bad day on the whole, though one on which the angler will probably save a blank, if he is lucky enough to be at a good place at the right moment. The best chance of having a really good day's sport is when the river has cleared after a flood and is falling. The salmon have then stopped running, but are not yet thoroughly settled in their new places. They are still active and alert and more ready to pay attention to salmon flies. I think it is probable, that the more recently a salmon has entered a pool the more likely it is to take a fly. It is not hard to imagine that the salmon is in good spirits at finding itself in an easy comfortable resting-place after struggling through rough water and over shallows. In spring, when the rivers are full and salmon can keep on moving up day after day without being dependent on a flood, I have noticed that a fish, which is seen to make a boil at the tail of a pool, frequently comes at the fly, if it is cast over the place directly or soon afterwards. A gillie of much experience, a very good fisherman, first called my attention to this, and said that he thought these were fish which had just entered the pool, and I think he was right.

Salmon fishing is a sport in which the angler need not grudge any amount of success either to himself or his friends, if they fish with a fly. In any fair-sized river, the number of salmon which can be caught with the fly even by fishing all day and every day up to the end of October, is so small in proportion to the whole of the fish, that the stock of salmon belonging to the river will never be impaired or unduly reduced in this way. The salmon which are in one proprietor's stretch of the river one day may not be there the next. He need no more think of sparing them, when they are inclined to take, than he need think of sparing woodcocks, when shooting his covers, in order to reserve them for another day's sport. In this respect salmon fishing has an advantage over trout fishing. The migratory habit of salmon gives a feeling of freedom to do one's utmost, as well as a feeling of uncertainty whether the fish are in the water or not.

But migration leads to great difficulties and draw-backs. If it is true that it is not in the power of any one owner to spoil his own and other people's sport by fair fly fishing, it is also true that it may be in the power of one owner by netting, to spoil the sport of the whole river, and as a matter of fact sport on most rivers is seriously interfered with by netting at the mouth or in the lower waters. The question is a very difficult one, and has led to much legislation and litigation. It is clear that everybody, from the fisherman in the sea to the owners of the spawning beds at the head of the river and in its tributaries, ought to have some share of the salmon, but I do not think that legislation has always managed to distribute this share fairly, or in a way which is satisfactory to the various interests, and is likely to protect the average stock of fish. I do not write as an expert in these matters, but it appears to me that on very many rivers the netting is too severe and too constant during the spring and summer, and that it might on the other hand be prolonged to a later date in the autumn. At present it often happens that anglers get practically no sport at all till the netting season is over, and it is becoming the habit of the salmon in some rivers to ascend them later in the season owing to the fact that year by year it is only the late running fish that have a free passage. This state of things is neither to the interest of the anglers nor of the netsmen. The nets get fewer fish because an increasing proportion of fish do not enter the river till after the netting season is over; the anglers have most of their sport crowded into the back end of the season, when the fish are not in first-rate condition; and the numbers and general quality of the stock of salmon in the river deteriorate. It would be much better for everybody, if the netsmen allowed a longer weekly close time in which salmon might run freely all through the season, and were in return given an extension of time in which to net fish at the end of their season. At present the netting season ends while the fish are still in first-rate condition at the mouth of the rivers. It ought not to be prolonged to the present date of the rod fishing, which now extends to the end of October or even November, but on most rivers there is now a margin of two months between the close of the netting, and that of the rod fishing. This margin might very well be reduced by prolonging the netting season in return for a guarantee that anglers should have a larger share of the spring and summer salmon.

Let us return, however, to angling proper. Next in

importance after the condition of the water comes the state of the weather. Everybody concludes that there is some connection between the state of the weather and the mood of the fish, but we have never been able to establish it scientifically. Perhaps some future generation will read another Blue Book, which will by chemical analysis explain the effect of the weather upon the mood of salmon, and enable us to arrange our angling accordingly. But at present it does not appear that the united experience and observation of all anglers, past and present, has been able to produce a satisfactory set of rules to guide us. Heavy warm weather, with low bits of cloud sulking about on the sides of the mountains, is generally very bad: a gale of wind is sometimes good, especially when the water is low: extreme heat is much worse than extreme cold. I do not think a high sun matters, unless the water is very clear and low, but I distrust a low sun shining right down a pool, full in the faces of the fish. The angler may be well content if there is a fresh feel in the air, and the clouds are light and high, but the first and last advice about salmon fishing is to work hard in any light, under all conditions of weather or water (except in a rising flood), whenever there is good reason to believe that salmon are in the river.

CHAPTER VIII

TACKLE

ANGLERS have sought out many inventions in tackle. Life is not long enough for us to be able to use more than a small portion of these, and it seems to me that the object of writing about tackle to-day should be to lessen and not to increase the amount which we think it necessary to carry with us. This is what strikes me when I reflect upon the enormous variety of flies described in books and displayed in tackle shops; and upon the consequent difficulty of making a selection for the outfit for an angling holiday: one cannot buy up the whole stock of salmon and sea trout flies, but as the eye dwells upon the patterns of flies, almost each in turn seems so attractive as to be indispensable. How often have I gone into a tackle shop to make provision for a spell of fishing in Scotland, and entered it with fairly distinct ideas of the limits, both in number and variety of flies that were wanted; and how often have these limits expanded and at last dissolved altogether under the genial influence of the display of flies upon the counter! The number of seemingly indispensable patterns increases as the sheets of flies are spread before me; so too does the number of seemingly indispensable sizes of each pattern, and at last I emerge, exhausted by the struggle of selection, alarmed at the amount of my purchases or my order, and yet uneasy for fear it should not be large enough and I should have omitted the one thing needful after all.

Now assuming for the moment that there ever is such a thing among salmon and sea trout flies as the one thing needful, it is true that the larger the collection of flies in the angler's box or boxes, the more chance is there of this one thing being included: but, on the other hand, it is also true that the very large extent of choice in his boxes diminishes the angler's chance of selecting the right thing at any given moment.   After much trouble I have therefore come to the conclusion, that we lose more than we gain by carrying about a large stock of fancy flies, and by this I mean that we lose not only in purse, but in number of fish.   I have come to believe that in all kinds of fly fishing we get most success on the whole by concentrating our attention upon a few patterns of proved merit and persisting with them, and my advice to every young angler is to get confidence in a few patterns by experience, as quickly as he can, and to stick to these.   He must at first use the experience of others to put him on likely tracks, but that confidence, which is half the inspiration of good fishing, must be gained at first hand.   Being convinced therefore that the object should be to exclude patterns of flies rather than to include them, and to lead us to concentrate upon a few varieties only in the virtue of which we thoroughly believe, let me give the results of my own experience, for what they are worth.

Of salmon flies I will give four patterns.

1. Jock Scott, as the best all-round fly, excellent for all seasons, weathers and waters in Great Britain, and to be used of all sizes. I believe the Jock Scott to be the best blend of colours that has ever been invented for a salmon fly.

2. Wilkinson. A large size for high-coloured water, and a very small size in low water and bright weather.

3. Black Doctor. First-rate in summer, if used of a small medium, or very small size in clear water.

4. The Torish, tied with a yellow and not a blue hackle. This is an excellent fly in spring, and as regards size, I have found it most successful on a No. 6/o Limerick hook, which corresponds to a No. 16 or 17 size of hook in the new scale. With a box of these four patterns, tied of, say, five different sizes varying from No. 8 up to No. 18 (new scale) Limerick hooks, I should feel perfectly content, as far as salmon flies were concerned, on the banks of any British water at any season. Perhaps a few flies of a larger size than No. 18 should be added for exceptional occasions. I agree, however, with the views which are so well expressed by Sir Herbert Maxwell with regard to salmon flies in his delightful book on salmon fishing, and am prepared to admit that there may be many other sets of four patterns of equal virtue. But the accidents of personal success have led me to fix upon these four, and therefore I give them in the belief that, though other patterns may succeed as well, none will do better.

For sea trout let me take the following:

1. Soldier Palmer.   I have found no better fly than this, when a river is in good order after a spate.   A good size is one tied on No. 8 Pennell-eyed Limerick hook, and this is the form in which I use it; its merits are not confined to sea trout, for in one day on a single-handed rod, while fishing for sea trout, I once landed five grilse, weighing altogether 28½ pounds, on this fly.   I do not think it has the same virtue in smaller sizes when the water is low and clear.

2. Jay wing, black body, ginger hackle, silver twist. This fly is not so good as the former in highly coloured water, but is most excellent and reliable in clear water; the size may be varied from No. 4 to No. 8.

3. Woodcock and yellow.   Succeeds in the same sizes and under the same conditions as the preceding pattern.

4. Black and orange spider.   I use this alone on a bright day and in low clear water, tied on a No. 4 Pennell-eyed Limerick hook, and have found it in these conditions attractive to sea trout and sometimes irresistible to herling.

In wet fly fishing for trout I am content with March-browns, Greenwell's glories, and Mr. Cholmondeley-Pennell's No. 1 hackle fly in spring, tied upon Nos. 1, 2, and 3 hooks.   As the season advances and the rivers become very low and clear, I change to a red quill gnat and a black spider upon No. 0 hooks.

With favourite dry flies I have dealt in a previous

The salmon flies just described represent the four patterns for which I have lately had a preference; but my preference for patterns has varied from time to time, and is based upon fancy rather than upon reason.

The size is, I think, more important than the pattern of salmon flies.

The larger size (8·0) is for big water in March: the smaller size ($1\frac{1}{2}$) is suitable for moderate water and warmer weather as in May. Between these two sizes are many intermediate sizes to be used as best suits the height and temperature of the water, the state of the weather, and the period of the season. As a general rule larger flies are best, when the water is very cold, but should be replaced by smaller sizes as the water and weather become warmer. In low water and in summer salmon do not despise things as small as trout flies.

With trout flies the pattern is more important, and there is much less variety of size than in salmon fishing. The two flies of the larger size (No. 1) shown here are of frequent use for wet fly fishing on English or Lowland Scotch rivers in the early part of the season; but smaller sizes and other patterns will be used as the season advances. If I were restricted to one size and three patterns only for dry fly fishing, the size should be oo, and I should rely upon a grey quill gnat in May and a red quill gnat in summer, with a black spider to be used as a surprise change for a good trout that obstinately refuses the winged flies. The black spider is also useful as a wet fly.

For sea trout and for Highland loch fishing larger sizes of flies are useful; but variety of patterns for all sorts of fly fishing can be studied and pondered in books more technical than this and on the counters of tackle shops.

Top—Mar Lodge (8·0).   *Bottom*—Delfur Fancy (8·0)

chapter, and I need only state their names here. They
are:

1. Olive quill—medium shade.
2. Red quill.
3. Iron blue.
4. Black Spider. Nos. oo and o Hall's eyed hooks
are useful sizes for all these.   A No. ooo red quill is
very successful in rising trout on hot midsummer days;
but it is too small to hold heavy fish satisfactorily.

As there is sometimes a difficulty in identifying flies,
I have in this case referred to Messrs. Hardy of Alnwick,
and have adopted their names or descriptions of the
patterns which I submitted to them.

Gut is the most troublesome of all parts of an angler's
tackle, but less so in the case of salmon and sea trout,
than in trout fishing.   I prefer in salmon fishing to have
a cast tapered with some three feet of plain single gut
next the fly, it is more transparent than any twisted gut
can be, and it is not difficult to get it round, clear and
strong.   The thickness of it must be proportioned to
the size of the fly, the size of the rod, and the strength of
the stream, rather than to the size of the fish.   Even a
big salmon in easy-going water can be landed on comparatively fine gut with a light rod, but a heavy rod and a
large fly are not compatible with fine gut.   No one can
play a fish so delicately with a big rod as with a small one,
and perpetual casting with a large fly soon wears out the
gut near its head—if fine gut is used.

For sea trout in clear water, when a single-handed rod
is used, a tapered cast ending in the finest undrawn gut
should be strong enough; be sure, however, that the gut

really is undrawn, and have some spare lengths of it with which to keep the finer end of the cast in repair.

It is a great pity that we cannot get undrawn gut fine enough for difficult trout fishing. The strength of new undrawn gut is, in proportion to its thickness, quite amazing and it will stand a great amount of wear and tear. It is when we come to drawn gut that our difficulties are so great. Like all gut it has an unruly curliness when it is new and dry; it begins to rot when it is kept wet or exposed; it frays and wears thin when it is used. Even when sound one often breaks it when testing it: if it is not tested, one cannot be sure that it is not rotten. All an angler can do is to keep a pretty fresh stock of drawn gut of different thicknesses, and put on the finest that he dares to use, and renew the fine end of his cast whenever he sees that it is getting weak and worn. It is well to remember also that the constitution of all gut, drawn and undrawn, differs: some casts, which are strong enough when new, rot much sooner than others. It may be that the amount of sunshine, or the sort of weather to which they are exposed, causes the difference. I prefer not to carry spare casts and gut damp, but to soak each new piece as it is wanted. This takes a little time, but not really very much, and I think that the less gut has been exposed to alternate moistening and drying before being used the better it is.

For knotting lengths of gut together the ordinary double knot is as good as anything. The single knot will hold if the gut has been properly soaked, but the gut will break at a single knot much more easily than at a double one. For tying small dry flies on to the end of the cast the Turle knot, as described in Mr. Halford's book, is the best and the generally accepted one; no angler need trouble about any other. For salmon flies on gut loops, I use the following knot: Pass the end of the gut *up* through the loop, bend it over on the further side, bring it under the loop and pass it up under itself so as to form a loop of its own round the fly loop. Then bend the end of the gut back over the cast, and pass it through its own loop, carrying it flat along the body of the fly, and pointing towards the bend of the hook. Then hold this end still while the knot is drawn tight. This is a most easy knot to tie, even with cold fingers; it is safe, and can be undone when the fly is changed.

Of lines it is only necessary to say that tapered waterproof plaited silk lines are excellent, but I think, at any rate for trout fishing, that nothing is better than a Manchester waterproof plaited cotton line; when it is new it goes into the eye of the wind beautifully. I think the silk line is better than the other after each has had a season's wear, but though lines, if carefully and regularly dried, will last a long time, they should be frequently tested and not trusted too long. A ludicrous accident once happened to me, when fishing for salmon with an old line. It was a pouring wet morning, and just at the critical moment when the river began to rise I hooked a salmon in a broad open stretch of water. This salmon played sulkily; after a few minutes I tried to reel in some line, but the fish was not very willing; the wet line would not run easily on the dripping rod, and broke suddenly about halfway up the rod. I was alone, but the fish, not understanding the situation, gave me time to lay down the rod, and knot the line rapidly to a ring. What I ought to have done of course was to join the two ends of line near the reel, and trust to being able to play the fish without needing more line than was already out: had I done this I should have retained for myself the privilege of being able to reel in line. But to do this would have taken longer, the fish might have made a bolt while I was doing it, and I was in great terror and had no time to reflect. The result was that when communications were re-established, I was attached to a salmon about twenty yards away, without any power either of reducing the distance, or of allowing it to be increased. Far below me was a broad extent of shingle, and I fought to gain this. The river was at least forty yards broad, but the salmon kindly restricted all his struggles to my side, and at last I stood upon the shingle, on a level with the water, and with flat ground on which I could retire from the water's edge. This I began to do, and was succeeding yard by yard when the hold gave and the fly came back to me. Then followed the thought of how much better things might have been managed, and the blank despair of knowing that with a rapidly rising river, there was no chance of another salmon that day.

On one other occasion my reel line broke. I had hooked a salmon, which ran up into some water full of notorious sunken rocks, among which the line got fast. I put on a strain in every possible direction, and tried pulling by hand, but could move nothing and feel nothing. As a last resource I let out all my line and went down to the full length of it in order to get a pull as directly down stream as possible. The line broke unexpectedly, close to the reel, and in a moment was swept out of the rings by the stream, and into the river, and I saw it no more that day. But the next morning my friend wading on the opposite side in slack water felt something round his feet, and at luncheon presented me with the whole of the lost line and part of the cast still attached to it.

The lines usually sold for dry fly fishing are, I think, made rather too heavy. It is well to have a heavy line ready for a day with a strong down stream wind, but the lines which are generally recommended for dry fly fishing seem to me not only heavier than is necessary, but heavier also than is pleasant or desirable for fishing in ordinary weather.

A very heavy reel line makes one's fishing less delicate, and on days when very fine gut has to be used, it makes what may be called the gradient of the taper too steep, so that the fly is continually catching the reel line in the air, and interrupting one's casting. By all means keep a reel with a heavy line in readiness, and in rough weather go out to contend against an adverse gale equipped with your stiffest rod and a heavy line and a short gut cast, but for ordinary days use a lighter line, and more gut even though you continue to use (as I do) a stiff rod.

For many years there has been a constant improvement proceeding in the make and pattern of reels; it is easy enough to get a good one, and every angler should get one of the best construction. It is better to have one good reel than two inferior ones, for an unreliable reel entails the certain loss of a big fish sooner or later. The line is sure to refuse to run at some critical moment, either because it has been overrun and tangled on the reel, or because the reel sticks suddenly. There should be no temporizing or working on with a reel which has once begun to play tricks; till it has been overhauled and made good, trust it no more than you would a watch which has taken to stopping at odd times.

For a first-rate rod it is generally agreed that there is a choice of two materials—greenheart and split cane. Nothing throws a better line, or is more pleasant to use than greenheart, but it has one disadvantage, that of being more brittle than split cane, and after breaking many greenheart tops I have taken to having split cane tops made for a greenheart salmon rod, and have found them last better. The cost of each top is only about thirty shillings, and a rod so composed is, I believe, about as strong as one entirely of split cane.

For double-handed trout rods I know nothing better than one entirely of split cane, and I prefer it with a steel centre.

For dry fly fishing and single-handed work it seems to me that a split cane rod is cheaper in the long run than any other. It should be in two pieces only, and in delicate work with a dry fly, I think that one can fish more accurately without a steel centre.

Every angler who has fished much on chalk streams must know how impossible it is even with the greatest care to prevent the hook touching or catching in weed now and then, when a line of any length is being lifted off the water quickly. Time after time have greenheart rods been snapped most untowardly in this way. Mine generally broke close to the joint, and years ago I took to diminishing the danger by using two-piece spliced greenheart rods. These were a little more troublesome to put together than the ordinary rods, but if they broke at all it had to be somewhere else than at the splice. Even these did not remove all danger of disaster, if, when one was working hard and keenly, the hook caught suddenly either in a weed in front or in a bush or grass behind, and at last after many accidents, partly caused by being, I fear, a somewhat hasty and too vigorous angler, I bought my first split cane rod, a powerful two-piece ten foot six rod, of Messrs. Hardy in 1884. The butt and joint of that rod are still as sound as ever, after landing many fish of all weights up to ten pounds, and though I have worn out one or two tops, not one has ever broken suddenly in the act of fishing, and they have stood faithfully against the most fearful shocks caused by weeds or bushes in the act of casting. It is this toughness of split cane which, in my opinion, settles the question decisively in its favour, and though after several seasons' hard work in all sorts of weather and in contending against down stream winds a split cane top may weaken, mine have always given me ample warning: never in trout fishing, since I have used split cane, have I lost a minute's fishing by the breaking of any part of my rod. Split cane is the most staunch of all materials; like an old and faithful servant, it is incapable of treachery or sudden change, and when it fails it does so gradually. My own original split cane rod has become a trusted companion, used to all winds and weathers, to burns, chalk streams and rivers of many kinds; to trout, sea trout and grilse; doing all that is asked of it, having more than once risen to the occasion of playing a salmon, and remained straight erect and fit after landing it.

After every season of hard work and exposure a split cane rod should be sent to its maker to be re-varnished, and the one or two split cane tops, which in the course of years I have thought it safer to lay aside, have failed owing to my having too often in the press of other things neglected this precaution. As there seems to be some controversy about the respective merits of greenheart and split cane, it may be worth while to add, that besides the ten foot six rod mentioned above, I have had two others of the same size built for my own use. The first of these did its work thoroughly, kept its straightness in spite of hard work, and lasted till I lent it to a friend, who rode with it on a bicycle along an open moorland road. Unfortunately, on the way he and the bicycle, with the rod tied across the handles, fell headlong down a grass slope, and the rod's life came to an end. I am sure that a two-piece greenheart rod would not have survived the fall either. The second was built to take the place of this broken split cane rod. It has done two seasons' fair work without a sign of weakness anywhere, and remains perfectly straight. After fifteen years' experience of single-handed split cane rods, I should without hesitation claim for mine that they have kept their straightness and lasted better than greenheart would have done under the same amount of work, and they have freed me entirely from the fear of a sudden break of the top joint in casting a line however long.

Years ago, when my wrist was young and weak, I found a difficulty in getting with one hand the full amount of work out of a ten foot six or eleven foot rod, which was powerful enough to throw a line against a strong wind, and I acquired as a boy the habit of fishing with the reel turned up and pressed against my arm above the wrist. This increases enormously the leverage which the arm has upon the rod, and I find that I can in this way fish easily with a rod which it would be quite beyond my power to use single-handed in the ordinary way for any length of time. I am bound to confess that I have not succeeded in inducing my friends to adopt this method, but I am convinced that it enables me to do more work with less weariness of the arm than would otherwise be the case, and that its advantage on the days when one has to contend with a strong down stream wind in dry fly fishing, is very great.

In all angling, but especially in dry fly angling, there is no greater misery than to be using a whippy rod. It never for a moment lets you forget its inefficiency: inaccurate even on still days, it seems to take a pleasure on rough days in watching the wind sweep away the line in the air, or blow it back. When you attempt to strike a fish, the silly top bends nearly to the water before it executes the strike, and when you have hooked a trout you are in despair at the rod's weakness and want of control. Take care, if a rod errs at all, that it does so on the side of stiffness.

So far this chapter has dealt only with the absolutely

essential parts of an angler's equipment. There remain other things of which some are indispensable on certain occasions, but not always, while others are merely convenient. Landing nets and gaffs present little difficulty whenever the angler has an attendant; but one of the great charms of angling is the complete independence which an angler feels when fishing alone, and never is this enjoyed more than when it is possible in salmon fishing. Unfortunately the conditions of salmon fishing make the constant assistance or advice of an attendant often indispensable. It is so when a boat has to be used, when the angler does not know the river, or when he has a reasonable expectation of landing more fish than he can carry home. There is, however, no more exhilarating experience, than when an angler, relying entirely upon his own knowledge and judgment, has risen and hooked a salmon, and has to face the struggle alone without the possibility of assistance of any kind. For these occasions, at any season of the year, when it is lawful, the angler who is alone should carry a gaff. Sir Herbert Maxwell describes in his book an arrangement for doing this, which I shall take the next opportunity of trying, for my experience hitherto has been that gaffs which are convenient to carry are not convenient to use, and those which are most effective in use are most awkward to carry. It takes longer to bring a salmon within reach of a gaff in one's own hand than it does to have it gaffed by an attendant; but if the hold of the hook is good the act of gaffing in ordinary water can be done as surely at last by the angler himself as by any one else, and the best way is the one which is most easy and certain—to gaff the fish over the back in the thickest part of the body.

But in gaffing my practice is the reverse of that when using a landing net for trout.   In the case of a fat lively trout on a small hook, the management of the rod seems to me up to the very end more difficult than the use of the net, and I therefore keep the rod in the cleverest hand—the right hand in my case.   I can receive a trout in the net and draw it to the bank as well with the left hand as with the right.   With the gaff it is not so; and at the moment of gaffing the management of the gaff is, I consider, more difficult than that of the rod.   My left hand cannot be trusted either to gaff or lift the salmon so surely as the other, and I therefore put the rod to the left hand as the critical moment approaches, and use the gaff with the right.   One ought, however, to be doubly sure that the fish is exhausted before trusting the rod to the left hand alone, and this is one of the reasons why it takes longer to gaff one's own salmon than to have it done by an attendant.

In trout fishing I do not like a net which must hang by the middle of the handle.   The net then hangs too low, and is more apt to catch in bushes, fences, brambles, or even under one's own feet when kneeling and crawling. There should be a hinge, not in the handle, but at the head of the loop of the net, which thus hangs by its head.   In this case the handle must be short, but if a longer handle is desired, a telescopic one may be used, with a metal clip so arranged that the handle hangs upright, but telescoped, on the strap of the basket, with the net folded over at the head.   This sort of net is easily detached, and the handle and net are both sent out straight in a moment with one movement of the hand.

The lightest and most comfortable form of waders for water meadows, or shallow water free from large stones or rocks, is that with long waterproof stockings coming well up on the thigh, and with indiarubber soled boots, the whole in one piece. These waders are not the most lasting, nor do they soon dry inside, but the convenience of being able to slip them on and off easily is very great. A heavier kind with more leather and nailed soles lasts longer. In salmon fishing, and in many trout rivers, wading trousers nearly up to the arm-pits, separate brogues and outside socks are needed. If one has to walk much from pool to pool they are a terrible discomfort. I hate the putting on of my wading trousers, the wearing of them, the walking in them, and the sight of them altogether, but I prefer them infinitely to fishing from a boat. They hamper one in every possible way, but they do not destroy one's independence.

As regards a fishing basket the only essential points are that it should be large enough and strong enough. Fishing baskets are made with all sorts of dodges, and every one can amuse himself by trying these, and may perhaps find some convenience in some of them. I have one basket which is fitted with so many dodges and straps, that though they were all explained to me once I have never been able to remember the use of all of them, and I sometimes spend idle moments on the bank trying to re-discover for myself the meaning of certain of the more mysterious straps: but the basket holds the fish very well. For a basket of any size it is very important to have a *broad* soft band across the shoulder, in order to guard against soreness and to diminish the aching and oppression caused at last by a heavy weight.

Spring balances (a small one for trout and a large one for salmon); boxes for flies (in the case of dry flies one in which the flies are kept loose in different compartments, and not fixed with their hackles pressed upon cork); a soft leather case for casts and gut lengths, with separate pockets; a knife with scissors; dull neutral-coloured clothes, and a soft hat, in which flies may be stuck when frequent changes are necessary, with a brim above which a cast can be wound—these complete my equipment for fly fishing.

Some innate conservatism lurking in me has prevented me hitherto from taking to the use of paraffin for dry flies. I do not defend myself, for I cannot prove that an oiled fly is less attractive to shy trout than a clean one; but I do not believe that—except on very wet days —I should land any more trout by using paraffin, and I know that whenever a suspicious trout refused my fly I should be wondering whether the paraffin was the cause of it. Well-made dry flies used to float very well before paraffin was adopted; they do so still; and I resent the intrusion of the odious little bottle and oil among my fishing tackle.

On the other hand, I am grateful for any preparation or any dressing which makes the reel line float upon the water. The sinking of the reel line is a great drawback in dry fly fishing. If the whole of the line which is cast upon the water continues to float upon the surface, the striking of a trout, or the lifting of the line and fly for the next cast, are made much easier, and the chance of the fly dragging is diminished. In wet fly fishing a reel line which will insist upon floating is a great nuisance, and the angler should have at least two lines ready for use, one for chalk streams and another for wet fly rivers.

CHAPTER IX

EXPERIMENTS IN STOCKING

I HAVE never had any opportunity of stocking water on a large scale, but I have made experiments in two ponds, and the results may be of use to others who have similar pieces of water, and may perhaps be interesting or suggestive to those who have more extensive opportunities and can compare my little attempts with larger ones.

The first experiment was made in a new pond, which was excavated in a clay soil. This pond had a bottom of nothing but clay, and was fed by a small trickle coming down an open ditch, which became, however, a rushing turbid flood of surface water after very heavy rain. The pond was some ninety yards long by twenty to thirty yards wide, and varied from two to six feet in depth. Some weed (*Chara fœtida*) appeared of its own accord, and there was a natural supply of fresh water shrimps.

In May 1887 about 200 yearling Loch Leven trout from Howietown were put into this pond. By the autumn of 1888 these had grown to be from six ounces to half a pound in weight; in June 1889 they averaged about eleven ounces; in the last half of August 1889 seven trout caught with a fly weighed eight pounds, or an average of over one pound apiece. In August 1890 eight trout caught weighed only seven pounds five ounces, and the average for the whole of the season was a little under one pound. This then appeared to be the limit of the average weight that the trout would attain if the pond were kept stocked.

In February 1890 I put in seventy-five two year old *Salmo fontinalis,* and with these I had an interesting experience in the first autumn flood in the following October. I had constructed a sort of wire trap below the pond, in the hope of catching in it any fish which left the pond during floods. It was a very imperfect affair, for it was quickly blocked by leaves and overflowed, but after the first flood in October we took thirty-nine *Salmo fontinalis* out of it and replaced them in the pond. As there were at most only seventy-five *fontinalis* in the pond, it was certain that more than half of them had made a determined effort to get down stream, and it is probable that several others, besides those recaptured, had escaped from the trap and gone away altogether. The number of trout in the pond was about double that of the *fontinalis,* and yet not a single trout was found in the trap—a striking illustration of the difference in the habits of the two species of fish and of the much greater difficulty of retaining a stock of *fontinalis.*

In May 1891 the *fontinalis* in the pond had reached a weight of fourteen ounces; whilst in August one of one pound one ounce was caught, and the last ever seen there was in September 1891. Out of the seventy-five *fontinalis* put in only seven were killed altogether, and the experiment has in consequence not been repeated.

In regard to trout, on the other hand, out of about

250 (including the 200 yearlings introduced in 1887) put in at various times up to 1892, nearly 100 have been killed with fly, and though many have doubtless escaped during floods, yet there still remain a few in the pond. No small trout have appeared, and it is clear that those which do remain are fish which have been put into the pond artificially and not reared in it naturally. The result altogether has been an interesting illustration of the migratory nature of *fontinalis* as compared with our own trout, and it should be added that though one or two of the *fontinalis* appeared for a year or two in the burn below the pond, and found their way into a larger burn well stocked with trout, yet none of them remained there, and they have, I believe, entirely disappeared.

My second experiment was tried in a different place which was originally a quarry. It has been disused for many years, and a natural spring has filled it with water. The place is about 200 yards in length and of varying width, but in no part more than twenty five yards from bank to bank. The depth of water on the deep side is over ten feet, and may be much deeper for all I know. The water is generally quite clear, and no rain ever dirties it, for there is no inflow except from the hidden spring, or springs at the bottom. There is no visible outflow, but the water after reaching a certain level must soak into the ground, and probably finds its way into the common covered drains of the field. There are two sorts of weed growing naturally in this water, one is *Chara fœtida*, which carpets the bottom and is full of fresh water shrimps, and the other is *Potomogeton natans*, a useless stringy thing, with leaves that cover the surface after the middle of July, and which has to be cut every summer in consequence. Into this place 200 yearling Loch Levens were put in May 1887. In the autumn of 1888 the weight of these varied from four ounces to three-quarters of a pound; in June 1889 those caught ran from eight ounces to fifteen ounces; in August one of one pound and a half was caught, whilst the nine fish killed in that month weighed ten pounds six ounces.

In February 1890 I added 100 two year old Loch Levens. These increased to three-quarters of a pound weight in 1891, and no more were imported into this water after 1890, for the trout have bred in it in spite of the absence of any stream. This seems to me an interesting fact, and it is one which, so far as this water is concerned, is beyond all doubt. In 1892 trout of about four ounces appeared in it; and I have a note to the effect that in 1894 "there are many fat and pretty half-pound trout, which rise freely." Those small fish, it is clear, could not be the two year old trout of 1890, for the latter had grown into mature fish of larger size in 1891; and if any doubt still remains it is surely disposed of by the fact that a record has been kept by me of the number of trout killed out of this water, and now amounts to 321 trout of three-quarters of a pound and upwards, against a total of only 300 trout introduced. It must be borne in mind also that my list of the trout killed is probably not complete, for some others, especially of the yearlings in 1887, must have been destroyed either by large gulls or herons, which occasionally visit the place, or by other methods which have not come under

Rainbow trout and bull trout

my observation. The secret of the breeding of those trout in still water is, I believe, to be found in the fact that there is a very small part of the pool joined to the rest in ordinary winters, but shut off from open connection with the main body of water in summer. The trout spawn on the stony shallow between the two pieces of water in winter. The ova hatch out, and such of the fry as have taken refuge in the small pool are shut in there, and thus protected from the larger fish when the shallow connection becomes dry in May or June. I have continually found this detached pool, which is only a few yards in length and breadth, full of small trout up to the size of yearlings in summer, and in the following year have noticed a large increase of small fish in the main water. After dry winters, on the other hand, when the shallow has remained dry and the connection with the little pool has never been properly established, there has been no increase of small trout. Ova have probably been laid and hatched on other stony shallows, but the fry having no sanctuary have no doubt been devoured by the large fish. One pound and three-quarters is the weight attained by the largest trout killed hitherto, and one pound and a half is a common weight.

An experiment was also made with *Salmo fontinalis* in the same place, and seventy-five two year olds were put into the water in February 1890. In July 1891 the weight of these ranged from half a pound to three-quarters of a pound, but their condition seemed much better in April than at any time afterwards. In June 1892 these *fontinalis* averaged from three-quarters of a pound to one pound, but they had deteriorated in shape and condition. On the other hand, they had evidently bred successfully, for several very fat little *fontinalis* of a quarter of a pound appeared. Up to the end of 1892 eleven of the original *fontinalis* had been killed, and since then I have never seen another in the water. Their disappearance is most mysterious. They cannot have escaped, for there is no outlet nor inlet above ground. It may be suggested that the water has been poached: if so, why should the *fontinalis* alone have been exterminated, while the trout and rainbow trout (to which I will come presently) have survived? There remains the choice of only two alternatives. Either the *fontinalis* have all died from some cause, which did not affect the other fish, or else they all, little and big, young and old, suddenly took to living at the bottom and resisting the temptation, not only of artificial flies, but of drop minnows and worms, with which experiments have been made in the hope of discovering them.

This disappearance of the *fontinalis* is as annoying as it is mysterious, for they were at first most handsome and attractive fish in outward appearance; their sporting qualities were excellent, their flesh brilliant in colour, and the flavour far superior to that of the ordinary trout.

I now come to the rainbow trout (*Salmo irideus*), of which one hundred two year olds were put into this water in February 1891. In 1892 a few were over half a pound in weight, in 1893 they were about three-quarters of a pound and rose fairly well. Since then they have not attained to more than one pound and a quarter in weight. They have risen badly, and their flesh though pink is inferior. Twenty of the full-grown rainbows have been killed altogether, but many more have been landed.   There appear to be a fair number in the water still, for they take a bait in the deep water better than a fly on the surface, and in more than one year, including 1898, small rainbows of a quarter of a pound and less have been caught, which proves that they too have bred successfully in the still water.   The general condition of the rainbows landed has been very inferior to that of the trout, but this is partly accounted for by the fact that they appear not to be in season during the best of the fly-fishing time.   My rainbow trout are full of milt and ova in April, and those we have caught in May and June—the best rising months—have not been fit to eat.

I feel that the value of all these experiments, and the inferences to be drawn from them, are restricted by the tiny scale upon which alone I have had any opportunity of stocking water, but the record of them may perhaps stimulate others to give the result of larger and more valuable experiences.   Both the *fontinalis* and the rainbow trout are such handsome fish, and have such sporting qualities, that I hope efforts to establish them will be continued for some time by experiments made in all sorts of water.

CHAPTER X

SOME MEMORIES OF EARLY DAYS

EVERY angler must have some account to give of the beginning of his keenness for angling. Some of us remember it as the great excitement of our boyhood, whilst others have only discovered its existence in later years of life. I think, however, that the keenest anglers are born and not made; that the passion is latent in them from the beginning, and is revealed sooner or later according to opportunity. In some cases it may be that the passion perishes unsuspected and unrevealed, because there is no opportunity of indulging or discovering it, till too late in life. The longer we live the deeper becomes the groove or the rut in which our life moves, and the more difficult it becomes to go outside it. To me the opportunity for fishing came early, and the passion for it awoke suddenly. I remember very well being seized with the desire to fish. I was about seven years old, and was riding on a Shetland pony by the side of a very small burn. A mill was working higher up the stream, and the water was full of life and agitation, caused by the opening of the sluice of the mill pond above. I had seen small trout caught in the burn before, but now, for the first time and suddenly, came an overpowering desire to fish, which gave no rest till some very primitive tackle was given me. With this and some worms, many afternoons were spent in vain. The impulse to see the trout destroyed all chance of success. It did not suit me to believe that it was fatal to look into the water before dropping a worm over the bank, or that I could not see the trout first and catch them afterwards, and I preferred to learn by experience and disappointment rather than by the short, but unconvincing, method of believing what I was told.

For some years this burn fishing was all that I knew. It was very fascinating, though the trout were so small that one of four ounces was considered a good one, whilst the very largest ran to six ounces. These larger trout taught me a second lesson—self-restraint. The first lesson was, as has been said, to learn to refrain from looking into the water before I fished it: all the trout of every size combined to teach this. The second difficulty was to restrain the excitement when I had a bite. The natural impulse then was to strike so hard as to hurl the fish into the air overhead: this answered very well with trout of two or three ounces, though once a small one came unfastened in the air, flew off at a tangent into the hay behind, and could not be found. But with six ounce trout this violent method did not answer so well; neither the angler, nor the rod, nor the tackle, was always strong enough to deal with them so summarily. Catastrophes occurred, and by slow degrees and painful losses I learnt the necessity of getting keenness under control. After I had improved in these matters there still remained the hardest trial of all, which has to be undergone by all anglers, namely, how to face the disappointment of losing a fish. Many of us must have known what it is in boyhood to suffer anguish after losing an unexpectedly large fish. The whole of life then seems laid waste by despair; the memory of past joys counts for nothing; one is sure that no future success can ever compensate for the present loss; and one rails against the established order of everything, and is indignant that any human being should ever have been born to undergo such intolerable misery. Even in later years we cannot hope to face the loss of very large fish with equanimity. Nobody can become perfect in bearing what is unbearable, and it may be counted to our credit if in these very bitter moments silence descends upon us, and we preserve outward appearances. Here is a saying that is very relevant: " When things can neither be cured nor endured, one has to pretend."

Burn fishing is not without its charm even in later years, and is a peculiar form of angling separate from all others. I am thinking now of those north country burns too small for fly fishing, which run in narrow stony channels between overgrown banks. Here one must fish with a worm and a short line, and the difficulty consists in getting the worm into the water without any part of oneself being seen by the trout. The usual method is to advance stealthily, sometimes stooping, sometimes on one's knees, sometimes at full length, according to the necessities of the case, pushing the rod in front, and at last swinging the worm gently on a short line over the edge of the bank and lowering it into the water. When the angler knows the burn well he goes at once from place to place, approaching the bank afresh at each spot which he knows to be suitable. If he does not know the burn he must reconnoitre from a distance to see the sort of water that is before him. It does not do to drop a worm blindly over the bank without knowing where it will fall, as the hooks are sure in this case to become mixed up sooner or later with a bush or a heap of sticks.

One burn I used to fish flowed through a wood of high trees down a steep rocky channel. Here it was possible, at least for a small boy, to keep out of sight by walking up the bed of the burn itself, stooping low, jerking the worm up into little pools and cascades above, and lifting the trout out down stream on to the bank. This was very pretty work. I remember once getting several trout quickly one after the other in this place, and then they suddenly stopped taking. One little favourite pool after another produced nothing, and a fear of something unknown came over me; the gloom and stillness of the wood made me uneasy, everything about me seemed to know something, to have a meaning, which was hidden from me; and I felt as if my fishing was out of place. At last I could resist the feeling of apprehension no longer; I left the rod with the line in a pool to fish for itself, and went up to the edge of the wood to see what was happening in the open world outside. There was a great storm coming up full of awful menace, as thunderclouds often are. It filled me with terror. I hurried back for my rod, left the burn and the wood, and fled before the storm, going slow to get breath now and then, and continually urged to running again by the sound of thunder behind me.

Burn trout are wayward little things. Sometimes they take a worm greedily on the brightest days in low clear water, rushing to it directly it falls into the pool, or seizing it as it travels down the stream, and being hooked without trouble. On these days all the angler need do is to wait for four or five seconds after he knows, by the stopping or the trembling of the line, that the worm has been taken, and then strike sharply but not violently. If the trout is very small it may be lifted out at once, but if it is four ounces' weight or heavier it is safer to let it do some splashing and struggling in the water, to wait till it is still, and then to lift it out with an even movement, quickly but without any sudden jerk. If there is a clear space without branches or bushes in the way, this can be done without the trout struggling in the air. It is always unsafe to lift a fish which is in the act of struggling, for the jerks of the fish, added to the dead weight of its body in the air, greatly increase the risk either of the line breaking or of the hooks coming out. If the trout exceeds six ounces, I play it with as much respect as if it were a salmon, and choose a shallow landing-place, and draw it on to that without lifting it at all. The feeling of losing a trout in the air is familiar to burn anglers. The fish falls back into the water with a splash, the line flies up into the air, often becoming hopelessly entangled in a tree; and before it is extricated the angler has frightened all the other fish in the pool, and is convinced that the trout and the branches and the rod and line and hooks are all in a conspiracy against him. I use the word " hooks," as I have found small Stewart or Pennell worm tackle much the best for trout fishing: it is easily baited, and with it the angler can, if he likes, strike directly the worm is taken, though it is better to wait just long enough to let the trout get all the worm well into its mouth, and not long enough to let the worm be swallowed.

On some days burn trout are very aggravating, and will take the worm and chew it without being hooked. The angler waits and then strikes, and feels that he has just touched a fish and no more, and this happens time after time. He tries the effect of waiting longer before striking, and then finds either that he still just misses the fish, or else that the fish has taken the worm off the hooks or has left the worm altogether; or that a very small trout not worth killing has swallowed the hooks, and wasted its own life and his time and trouble. I suppose on these days the trout are not really hungry, and begin to chew the worm instead of trying to swallow it at once. They then discover the presence of the hooks, and either reject the whole thing, or try to separate the worm from the hooks with their lips, which results in the angler's touching without hooking them when he strikes. There are other days when burn trout dash at the worm and endeavour to make off with it immediately at speed. On these occasions the angler feels a quick tug and all is over before he can strike; he probably does strike too late, and his line having no resistance at the end is jerked out of the water into a bush, if there is one near.

Three other moods are common to burn trout; they are those of indifference, suspicion, and abnormal fright. When the trout are indifferent, they simply ignore the worm, and appear not to notice its presence: one might think from their behaviour either that they were blind, or that they habitually lived with worms before their eyes. When they are suspicious, they will, on the contrary, swim up to the worm and investigate it as if they had never seen such a thing before, or dash about it as if its presence excited them. On other days, and these are not necessarily the brightest, it is almost impossible to keep out of sight of the trout, which seem to be watching for the least hint of the approach of an angler; and even when the angler succeeds in concealing himself, they fly from the sight of the rod, or the gut, however quietly it is put before them. All these things make burn fishing an interesting and delicate sport. The drawback to it is that the constant stooping and crawling become so much harder as years go on. Joints ache and crack, and the continual effort of keeping a stiff and full-grown body out of sight is difficult and painful. Some of the crouching may be avoided by using a long rod, but among bushes and trees a long rod is an awkward instrument, and one cannot guide the line so accurately among the branches. To dodge bushes and leaves and twigs successfully, the angler must use a short stiff rod and a short line. He can then not only guide the line and drop the worm more accurately with the rod, but after fishing each place can catch the end of the short line with one hand, while still holding the rod with the other, and so make his way through the trees to the next pool, without having to put the rod down and alter the length of the line. A well wooded burn is the nicest of all. It has places where the angler can watch the trout and see his worm taken, while he is hidden behind leaves, or lying in tall meadow-sweet or some such undergrowth of herbs. Even if he does not feel the thrill and the rapt excitement, which he felt as a boy when his line stopped and trembled in the stream with a bite, or when he saw a trout open its mouth and take his worm, he can still remember what he used to feel in those early days, and "beget that golden time again." He can enjoy, too, more than he ever did before, the light playing through the leaves upon the still water of a clear pool, the running water sparkling in the sun, the tinkling sound of little streams, and the shade and the hot summer's day. And even yet there is some satisfaction, when the burn is low and clear, in outwitting the trout, small as they are, for it is not to be done without care, difficulty, and effort.

I need hardly add that fine drawn gut is proper for burn fishing: in small burns two or three feet of gut is enough, as the water is shallow, the line is kept more perpendicular than horizontal, and but little of it falls into the water. The special merits of brandling worms were so impressed upon me from the first that I have never been content to use any other kind. They are certainly good both in colour and size. The objection to them is that they are rather soft, but for burn fishing, where the worm is dropped rather than cast into the water, this does not matter so much. Brandling worms, however, are not to be found in common earth, nor in every heap of decaying manure or rubbish. Kitchen garden refuse is a valuable ingredient, but it is not the only one, and the heaps must be of the right material in the right stage of decay; young anglers of intelligence and observation make it their business to know the best places for brandling worms, so that they may be sure of getting a good supply whenever they want it. The brandlings are best after being kept for a day or two in clean moss, but trout take them well enough when they are fresh.

Very wonderful is the perspective of childhood, which can make a small burn seem greater than rivers in after life. There was one burn which I knew intimately from its source to the sea. Much of the upper part was wooded, and it was stony and shallow, till within two miles of its mouth. Here there was for a child another world. There were no trees, the bottom of the burn was of mud or sand, and the channel was full of rustling reeds, with open pools of some depth at intervals. These pools had a fascination for me, there was something about them which kept me excited with expectation of great events, as I lay behind the reeds, peering through them, and watching the line intently. The result of much waiting was generally an eel, or a small flat fish up from the sea; or now and then a small trout, but never for many years one of the monsters which I was sure must inhabit such mysterious pools. At last one evening something heavy really did take the worm. The fish kept deep, played round and round the pool and could not be seen, but I remember shouting to a companion at a little distance, that I had hooked a trout of one pound, and being conscious from the tone of his reply that he didn't in the least believe me, for a trout of one pound was in those days our very utmost limit of legitimate expectation. There was a mill pond higher up in which such a weight had been attained, and we who fished the burn could talk of trout of that size, and yet feel that we were speaking like anglers of this world. But this fish turned out to be heavier even than one pound, and when at last it came up from the depth into my view, I felt that the great moment had come which was to make or mar my happiness for ever. I got into the shallow water below the fish, and after great anxieties secured with the help of my hand a fresh run sea trout of three pounds. Never was a dead fish treated with more care and honour. It had swallowed the hooks, and rather than risk spoiling its appearance in getting them out, the gut was cut and they were left inside. The small trout and eels and flounders were turned out of my basket and put into my companion's, so that the great sea trout might lie in state. It was felt that the expectation of years was justified, that the marvellous had become real, that the glory which had been unseen was revealed, and that after the present moment the hope of great things in the future would live for ever. A few years ago there was published a delightful book called *The Golden Age* in which the author describes the world of childhood as it has been to all of us—a world whose boundaries are unknown, where everything is at the same time more wonderful and more real than it seems afterwards, and where mystery is our most constant companion. So it was with me, especially in the places where I fished. I used to go to the lower part of this burn in the charge of an old gamekeeper, and after a long journey through pathless open fields, we seemed to reach a distant land where things happened otherwise than in the world nearer home. At the end of the walk it was as if we had reached another country, and were living in another day under a different sky. The gamekeeper fished more leisurely than I, and sometimes he would be lost among the windings of the burn, to be found again by the sight of the smoke from his pipe rising gently from behind a whin bush. When I now recall that distant land, I see always somewhere among the whin bushes a little curl of thin smoke, and no other sign of an inhabitant.

In course of time there came experience of a fine Highland river, and lochs near it and of fly fishing in them in August. The trout did not always rise very well in August, but many of them were three-quarters of a pound in weight, a few were even larger, and the sport seemed to me magnificent. Three great days happened all in different years on this river and its lochs. Once the trout took exceptionally well in the loch, and instead of the usual number of twenty or less I landed forty-eight, averaging about three to the pound. Another day there was a little fresh water in the river, and I tried an artificial minnow. First a trout of about two pounds, larger than any trout ever hooked by me before, was lost. While I was still in the agony of disappointment, a second weighing three pounds and a quarter was hooked and eventually landed, and directly after that a third trout of about the same size was hooked and lost, when it was in full view and half in the landing net. Then nothing more would take, and I spent the rest of the day without further incident, trying to think of the fish landed and not of the ones lost.

But the greatest day of all was the third. I was standing at the end of a pier built for salmon fishing, casting out into the smooth strong stream, when a sort of wave seemed to come suddenly and swallow the top fly, and a large heavy body went down stream pulling out the line. I shouted, "A salmon!" and the old gillie came hurrying to my side. His first words were, "We shall never get him," against which I protested with rage, and he partially retracted and set to work to advise me. We could not follow the fish downward, but it hove to about twenty yards below us and hung steady in the stream. We turned the trout rod up stream and held it still, keeping a steady strain upon the fish, and waited for what seemed an age without result; but the good old man encouraged me when I grew faint-hearted, and kept me patient. Eventually the fish began to yield. We gained line foot by foot, and more than once got the fish up stream nearly opposite the pier, but it saw us and dropped back each time to the old place down stream. At last amid great excitement it was coaxed past the pier, in a moment was in the backwater above, and to my astonishment was then almost at once exhausted and landed. It was a grilse of about six pounds, and rather red, but the distinction between grilse and salmon, between red fish and fresh run fish, was nothing to me. That same day another grilse of about four pounds took the same fly. This second fish took with a splash, ran freely and was landed without difficulty. In the course of many seasons I must have had dozens of days' trout fishing in that same river at the same time of year, but never on any other day did I hook or even rise a grilse or salmon with a trout fly.

These were the triumphs of luck, but they came at an age when youth, not from conceit, but from sheer gladness and simplicity, does not discriminate between luck and skill. The first temptation to become proud of possessing skill came later, and after the use of the dry fly had been learnt at Winchester. It was not on the Itchen that any pride was felt, for I was only a learner there, improving year by year, but with examples of greater skill and success than mine constantly before me. In the holidays, however, I took away with me from the Itchen to distant rivers the art of the dry fly, which was then not nearly so widely known as it has come to be in the last twenty years. So it happened that on west or north country streams, or in Ireland, or on dark smooth water in the Highlands, I was sometimes the first to introduce the dry fly, with results which astonished the trout and the local anglers, and were very gratifying to myself. In the Highland river spoken of above there was a long dark stretch, bordered by rocks and trees, where the river flowed with a deep even stream, carrying a few thin flecks of slow-moving foam upon its surface, but without a ripple. Here, especially in the evening, some of the best trout in the river used to rise. You might fish every day for a week in the rougher water and never hook a trout of one pound weight with a fly and be very grateful for half-pounders, but in this smooth deep part many of the trout were upwards of one pound, and the average weight was about three-quarters of a pound. Often had I tried them with March-browns, and small Heckum Peckums and the various patterns which are attractive in the Highlands, but not one of these particular trout would stand the sight of my flies. I continued to visit that river in my summer holidays, and the time came when I brought with me some drawn gut, some small olive and red quills, and a single-handed rod with which to cast them lightly. A pupil on the Itchen was a master among these Highland trout, and in the still hour of sunset on many an August evening I used to endure the torment of the midges and find a rich reward. A struggle with a trout of one pound and a half hooked on Itchen tackle in that fine flow of deep water, among the rocks and trees, was no mean affair.

In the Easter holidays I went alone once or twice to the Dart. I do not know how the Dart fares now, for it is nearly twenty years since I have seen it; but in those days there was beautiful trout water between Staverton and Buckfastleigh, which could be fished by ticket, and if one was not disappointed with trout of less than half a pound, there was very good sport to be had. I remember once fishing a part of the river where there was a succession of streams, which towards the middle of the day seemed alive with little trout, rising actively all over the water at natural flies. It was one of those maddening days when the trout rise in quantities and take no notice of artificial flies. I could do nothing, and the other anglers above and below me, of whom two or three were in sight, were not doing very much better. At last in despair I waded to the bank, and went down to a smooth piece of the river between wooded banks. In this place the water was clear, and varied from a foot to perhaps three feet in depth. No one was fishing, and there were trout rising in shoals and very quietly. A stout March-brown, such as I had been using above, would have put them all to flight, but the trouble of using a dry fly for each separate trout seemed out of proportion to the size of the fish. Yet as I wanted very much to save an empty basket, I gave up the hope of counting trout that day by the dozen, put on one small olive quill and waded in quietly below the rising fish. They took the little dry fly as if they were pleased to see it, and when the rise was over I waded out with thirty-one trout in my basket. The old angling diary to which I have referred gives the weight of the largest as eight ounces. It does not give the total weight, but I remember congratulating myself on the fact that the average size of my trout was at least equal to the size of those generally caught with fly in April in the more favourite streams above. As I emerged from the trees on the bank, I met one of the best of the local anglers returning from above with a lighter basket than usual. He stopped me and asked what I had done. I told him, and he then asked to see the fish. I opened my basket. " You can't have caught those to-day with fly," he said. " Yes," I replied; "I caught them with a dry fly." " Dry fly," he said very sternly, "we know nothing about a dry fly here." Then he went on his way, with thoughts, I fear, that were not very kind.

The next reminiscence goes back to about 1880, and has to do with a river in Ireland. The first time I saw this river was late in August. There were said to be trout, and good ones, and it was believed to be possible to catch some with fly earlier in the season, when the water was in order. The river had in parts a very wide bed, which when low it did not nearly fill. The water ran in all sorts of channels between beds of bright green weeds. Here and there was a long stream with a stony bottom, free from weeds, and now and then there would be a huge pool, full of peaty-coloured water of unknown depth, in which one or two salmon lay. One could wander for miles all day about the most extraordinary variety of water. The river was full of pike, and it was said, probably with truth, that the inhabitants of the district forked trout out of the weeds in low water with various agricultural implements. But there were trout enough for dry fly fishing. Half a dozen or so might be found rising near together, and then perhaps one would have to go several hundred yards before another one was found; a little sound would be heard presently, as if a small pebble had dropped in somewhere without a splash, and heard perhaps two or three times before the rise could be seen in such a large and curious river. Then there was a difficult stalk, probably through water and weeds, with the chance of going overhead into a big hole unawares.

I was warned that at this season of the year, when the water was low, I must not expect to catch any of these fish, but I cared nothing for warnings. The trout were there, and were rising, and though I saw at once that it was a case for dry fly and for that only, I had by this time been taught to believe that any one, who could catch

Winchester trout, could catch rising trout anywhere.
These trout, however, at first upset my calculations.
They brought me face to face with a difficulty which did
not exist on the ticket water at Winchester—they were
unapproachable. Never was an angler more put upon
his mettle. There were trout visibly and audibly rising,
which had never seen an artificial dry fly, and would
probably take it at once. They were evidently also big
trout. There was splendid sport to be had, and reputation and glory to be won in catching even one of them,
and yet so shy were they, that I could not get my dry
fly to them.

For two days they defeated me utterly. I walked and
knelt and waded and laboured and perspired under an
August sun without success. Some of the trout were
put down by my approach, some were scared by the first
waving of the rod, and some, which had been successfully
stalked, turned tail and fled when the gut floated over
them without even the least drag; at last, on the second
evening in a fading light, I hooked a fish which went off
up stream at once with a mighty rush, and came to rest
somewhere out of sight at the end of a lot of line. I
waded carefully up in the twilight, keeping a tight line
by reeling up as I went till I was over a great bed of
strong weeds. Into this one hand carefully felt its way
along the casting line, and touched at last the side of a
great fish. Nothing could be seen for it was getting
dark, and the weeds were too thick for a landing net to be
used in them. I tried with one hand to arrange a grip on
the trout, and very broad and hard he felt; but at the
critical moment he made the most violent commotion

in the weeds and dashed off somewhere. When all was
still I felt again and found in the weeds only the end of
broken gut. There was nothing more to be done that
evening, and I waded out and lay on the bank in the
dusk. On the whole, I think that was the bitterest
moment I have ever known in angling. To have come
so near to success, and to have it snatched from me at
the last moment, after keenness and effort had been
sustained at the very highest pitch for two whole days,
was more than could be borne.

But success did come afterwards, and in broad daylight; I found a place where, by wading and kneeling in
the river on the shallow side, it was possible to get
within reach of and *opposite* to rising trout without
frightening them. Then the fly could be thrown some
way above them with an underhand cast, so as not to
show the rod; and being opposite and not below, I could
let the fly float down a few inches on the near side of a
rising trout, so that only the fly and none of the gut was
seen. In this way I at last caught one or two trout, and
then somehow, when the frost of failure had once broken
up, it seemed more easy to succeed all over the river.

These trout were the shyest I have ever known. They
were more difficult to approach and more easily scared
by rod or gut than any others I ever fished for; but if the
fly could be floated to a rising fish without frightening
it, the fly was generally taken. On the best day that I
had there I caught eleven fish. None of these weighed
three pounds, but the first two were each over two
pounds and three-quarters. For such shy fish really fine
gut had to be used, and there were many disasters in the

weeds, but also many splendid struggles fought out in pools which were far too deep for any vegetation. It was the wildest and most exciting and most fascinating dry fly fishing that I have ever had. My experience of it has only been during late August or early September, but I can imagine that in May and in June it might be the finest dry fly fishing in the United Kingdom.[1]

[1] The river was the Suir, and the part of it described was at Graiguenoe, not far from Thurles. Before 1880 I do not think any one had ever fished it with a dry fly. I was never there after 1886, but I heard that the merits of the water for dry fly fishing were afterwards much appreciated by many anglers.

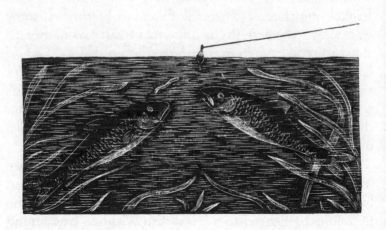

CHAPTER XI

SPRING SALMON FISHING—THE CASSLEY

It is interesting, but very strange, to read a book that was written by oneself more than thirty years ago. After such lapse of time the author reads it as if he no longer had responsibility for the book; it is to him now almost as if it were the work of some one else. Such is the feeling with which I have read through *Fly Fishing* with a view to the publication of a new edition, separate from and independent of the series of books to which *Fly Fishing* was originally my contribution. I have not attempted to revise the book, to prune or add or modify; or in any way make it the sort of book that I should write now. Here and there an ambiguous sentence has been made plain or the grammar corrected; and occasionally a note has been inserted to give the name of the river or pool in which some incident happened. But with these small exceptions the book remains as it was written years ago.

Some criticism it received at the time. One friend told me that he found the introduction "too philosophical," and that he did not propose to go on reading the book. From another quarter I heard of the negative and chilly commendation that the book was at any rate free from any "taint of whisky." But the reception it met with generally was much more favourable than I had dared to expect, and the fact that favourable reference is still made to it now and then is very gratifying.

The impression left on me after reading *Fly Fishing* again is that it is a happy book, and with this comes the sad reflection that I could not now write in this vein. At sixty - eight there is the sense of having "Kept watch o'er man's mortality," that was scarcely felt at thirty-six years of age. This is the common and inevitable lot of us all, but for the purpose of writing about angling there is now in my case a special personal disqualification. To write with briskness and buoyancy of spirit about our pleasures it is necessary to have prospect as well as retrospect. So it was when *Fly Fishing* was written: the days recalled or described were in thought the forerunners of numbers of angling days as good or even better that were still to come. My failure of sight is by itself sufficient to put an end to that prospect for me, as will be explained presently.

In fact, though I could not know this at the time, the best of my trout fishing was already over when *Fly Fishing* was being written in 1898. Seven years indeed of freedom, or at least of freedom in comparison with what followed, were still to come; but I do not recall any really great days of trout fishing in that period; nothing, for example, in the same class as the memorable day in the third week of July 1892, when six brace of trout were caught on the Itchen that weighed within a few ounces of 24 lb., and none of these were taken on large flies in the dusk. Nothing larger than oo size was used, and four brace of the trout, weighing a little over 17 lb., were caught during the morning rise before two o'clock in the day. The water —the Avington water on the Itchen—that I continued to fish was the same, but I do not recall any great achievements between 1898 and 1905, though I had some good days in every season. In the last of these years (1905) the trout never attained that superb condition which an Itchen trout should have. This was probably due to some temporary failure of food supply, such as fresh water shrimps, for the trout recovered again in a year or two; but their lack of condition in 1905 impaired the enjoyment of that season. For the angler who knows what a chalk stream can be becomes an epicure in his sport and cares to spend his skill only upon the best; and the difference in vigour and strength between a chalk stream trout in first-rate and one in poor or even second-rate condition is very disheartening to an angler who hooks the inferior fish.

For eleven years after 1905, at week-ends and for a few days at Whitsuntide, I dragged the weary clog of office work to the Itchen. The enjoyment of leisure is heightened by the contrast of work; this was so when I was an Under - Secretary from 1892-5. The work was arduous during the week, but when I left the office for a week-end in the country responsibility and work were left behind. But when Secretary of State, if I left London on Friday evening, I took a pouch of unfinished work with me, another pouch of work that had not reached me on Friday came on Saturday, and another pouch on Sunday morning. Even so, it was not lack of time that spoilt the fishing. It was not my custom on the Itchen to fish on Sunday, and in ordinary weather in May three or four hours from ten or eleven o'clock in the morning onwards will give the best that is to be got out of the day for dry fly fishing. To this in June may be added two hours more from seven to nine o'clock in the evening.[1] Dry fly fishing on a chalk stream does not demand the whole day, as do some other forms of sport, and my cottage was within a hundred yards of the river, so that I could go out or come in at any time. There was, therefore, time to fish and to work. But there was not the detachment or freedom of mind that are essential for zest and keenness, and my baskets of trout compared poorly with those of years that had been more free.

For two years after the Government, of which I was a member, resigned, the war still threw its dark shadow over everything, and when the war was over my sight had so failed that dry fly fishing had become impossible.

On this subject, therefore, I have nothing more to say: the best was over, and had been told when *Fly Fishing* was written. After that date also I had few opportunities of sea trout fishing, and not one good day.

Of spring salmon, happily, there are more and better things to tell. I came at last to know part of a salmon river really well, and to understand that without this knowledge the full joy of salmon fishing cannot be known. Anticipation, the knowledge of what to hope for or to expect, is an important factor without which the fullest pleasure cannot be. Every one must have

[1] Real sun time, not artificial "summer time."

felt how depressing is apprehension of future trouble or pain. Poets in melancholy mood dwell upon it. "We look before and after," says Shelley, and "Forward though I canna' see, I guess and fear," wrote Burns; but the looking forward to great pleasure increases happiness as much as the apprehension of pain depresses it. The prospect of salmon fishing in an unknown or little-known river is good, but it is much better when we can in imagination fish the pools beforehand, dwelling with the mind's eye on what experience has told us is the best spot in each pool.

In 1903 the lowest part of the Cassley was let to me for the month of April by the late Mr. W. E. Gilmour, the owner of Rosehall. In that year, and the two that followed it, my wife and I spent each April on the Cassley, and became much attached to it. After her death and my entry into office I did not visit the Cassley for two years. My brother fished it in 1907, and in subsequent years, till 1926 inclusive, fished it with me whenever he was in England in the spring. He became very fond of the river. He was by temperament, that is to say by keenness of spirit combined with coolness of head, and by natural aptitude for skill, a first-rate angler, and notably successful wherever he fished. Early in the war he lost his left arm close to the shoulder, but this did not impair his success in angling, though in salmon fishing he needed the help of a gillie to use a landing net or gaff. In dry fly fishing for trout he continued to fish unattended, being able by clever management and arrangements to land his own trout and put on eyed flies with one hand. He was also in angling, as in other matters, most considerate of others, and unselfish.

One cannot indulge one's own desire to describe a special place without risk of wearying those to whom it is unknown; but even at this risk I would give some description of a place which is endeared by such angling memories. The Cassley comes from the region of Ben More in Sutherland, and some account of the country and its sport may be found in a chapter of Charles St. John entitled "Life at Rosehall." The river runs at a right angle into the head of the Kyle of Sutherland, a long narrow piece of level water that goes inland from Bonar Bridge to the mouth of the Oykell. The tide comes to the head of the Kyle, but the upper part of it, at any rate, is not salt water. It was up the Kyle of Sutherland that St. John went in his amphibious conveyance, a boat with detachable wheels, to start on his tour in Sutherland.

After a course of some miles in an open channel, through moor or soft ground, the Cassley enters a narrow gorge about a mile before it gets to the bridge at Rosehall. The pools in this gorge are deep, dark, and interesting to look upon, but only once in April did we see a sign of a fish in these pools; it was a clean fish, but was not in the water, but on a rock at the edge, where no doubt it had been put by an otter, for a piece was eaten out of it. Some way down the gorge is a formidable waterfall, broad and steep, and below it a great pool— a typical Falls pool—and a very fine one for a river of such moderate size. Only in low water and in precociously warm weather do salmon ascend into this pool in April. Occasionally, but not often, we got a fish in it. When fishing is not productive it is pleasant to lie in the warm April sun at the edge of the trees on the top of the high bank on the left-hand side of the river, and to look down upon this pool; for it is a fine, fascinating, and beautiful place. Poets under such benign influences of Nature are moved to soothing thoughts of how life may end. Keats' thought was

> To cease upon the midnight with no pain

while listening to the song of a nightingale. Shelley's imagination was that death like sleep should steal upon him by the seashore, where he might

> hear the sea
> Breathe o'er my dying brain its last monotony.

Most peaceful of all is Wordsworth's description of the actual close of the life of an old clergyman in the Lake country. He was still able-bodied and hale, though in extreme old age, when—

> Like a shadow thrown
> Softly and lightly from a passing cloud,
> Death fell upon him, as reclined he lay
> For noontide solace on the summer grass,
> The warm lap of his mother earth.

So to one whose work was done and whose strength had failed might the end come fitly and happily while he lay listening to the sound of the falling water, his last sight that of the splendid pool with the sun shining on it, and his closing thought the exceeding beauty of the world in which he had lived.

From the Falls Pool the river makes a steep and rough descent, its course impeded by great rocks. On the top of one great rock, which stands up high in midstream, grows a Scots fir tree. In a narrow cleft on the bare top of this rock a pine seed must once have germinated and put up a shoot that has become a small sturdy tree. There can be no nutriment for its root except such of its own pine needles or other chance leaves that the wind has blown into the small cleft. There is nothing visible except bare rock to nourish its life. In all the years that I have known the Cassley this tree has held its own. It is stunted in growth and of small stature, but has asserted its right to be a tree. Its needles have a yellowish tinge, as if its complexion were sere from hardship. Drought has not starved it, nor flood overwhelmed it, though in big spates I have seen the spray reach it. It has not thriven, but it has lived, and it stands there on a bare rock, isolated by rushing water, an embodiment of dogged determination to demonstrate its right and power to live, where life seems impossible. Year after year I visited the place expecting to find it dead or gone; but always it was there unchanged and undaunted, and I paid a silent tribute of admiration to its hardihood.

At the end of this steep descent are the lower falls, as formidable to salmon as the upper falls; indeed, one would be disposed to say that both falls were impracticable for salmon but for the fact that salmon do ascend them. For sea trout apparently the falls are impracticable. There is no great wide pool under the lower falls; the water hurries away in a deep narrow channel, with high steep rock on the left side, till this rock terminates abruptly and the river takes immediate

The Scots fir on the rock (moonlight)

opportunity to turn to the left in the direction of the
quiet Kyle for which it is bound.   At this point floods
have hollowed out a piece of soft moorland bank on the
right side, and have made a large dark pool; but this side
of the pool is out of the current and of no use for
fishing: except that in very high water a side stream is
formed that runs along the right bank, and often gives
a fish, when the main stream is a raging torrent.   Near
the end this pool is narrowed again by a ridge of grey
rock that projects from the right bank, and on its upper
side stands sheer above or almost overhangs the black
water.   This ridge was known to us as the "goat rocks,"
and came by this name for the following reason.   In
April 1919 a friend and contemporary was fishing the
Cassley with me.   At Winchester he had excelled both
in cricket and football, but advancing years had cur-
tailed his physical activity.   When invited by the gillie
to go out upon this narrow ridge he flatly refused, saying
indignantly, "Do you take me for a goat?"

Nevertheless, it is easy to get on to the neck of the
ridge, and not difficult to get along the narrow top to the
tip of it, where the angler has just enough footing to be
able to stand and to cast.   From this point of vantage
the tail of the pool fishes best.   It is not a pleasant place
from which to play a fish: the angler cannot move; the
fish comes up into the deep still heart of the pool, and in
this a fish has once, at any rate, broken my cast round a
hidden rock.   In any case the angler must play the
salmon, unable to move himself, and standing high
and directly above the fish—always, in my opinion, an
unsatisfactory position—which puts a great strain upon

the rod. But when the fish is tired and under control, it can be steered into a narrow quiet inlet of water on the down stream side of the rocky ridge, and easily netted by a gillie. Even when alone it is not difficult for the angler to net his own fish; for on the down stream side the ridge, though it is too steep to be climbed, is not sheer, and the angler can slither down to the inlet and net his own fish.

I wonder whether the extremes of anxiety and emotion through which I pass when fishing alone for salmon are common to all anglers in like circumstances. The first impulse after hooking a salmon is to long for a gillie; then as the difficulty and anxiety of the contest with the fish develop, I curse my own rash and over-weening ambition that has deliberately deprived me of the advantage of the presence of a gillie, and thus increased the risk of not landing the fish; a contingency too intolerable to be borne, or even to be contemplated without dismay. Finally, when all has gone well, when the salmon has been tailed in shallow water, or netted and is safely on the bank, comes with a rush an all-pervading sense of exultation and exaltation, all regret and anxiety that have been due to the want of a gillie are submerged and obliterated by a great tidal wave of triumph. It is a supreme moment when the angler, having got the salmon on its side in shallow water or on shingle, and taken it by the tail, retires from the water to a safe distance, carrying the rod in one hand and the fish in the other. Then, indeed, he is as glad that he had not the help of a gillie as Henry the Fifth was glad that there was not one man more with him at Agincourt. Only when the angler is alone can he know to the very utmost the extremes of anxiety and triumph that salmon fishing can cause. It is, however, only on a river that the angler knows really well, and on which no boat is needed, that he can fish without the constant attendance and help of a gillie: even on the Cassley it was not my rule till my brother lost his arm and became more dependent on the devoted attendance of Angus Russ than I was.

One or two reflections that are the result of fishing unattended for salmon may be given here.

The angler should provide himself with one of the short sticks, metalled and heavy at one end, with which to dispatch the fish by a single blow on the head directly it is landed. It is a pity to leave the salmon gasping and flopping, while the angler searches for a suitable stone with which to knock it on the head. The fly is then taken out at leisure, and the fish can be admired as it lies on shingle, grass, or heather. In spring salmon fishing I do not myself use a gaff, but a landing net, so that the superb appearance of a fresh run salmon may not be marred by any wound. A gaff is, however, by much the quicker and more effective instrument, and on rivers where the angler is dependent upon a gillie, the latter must be left to use the instrument to which he is accustomed.

Is there any landing net that can be both easily carried and be really efficient when used, as it must be, with one hand by the angler himself? If there is, I do not know it. The handle must be short or it will not be easily carried: if the net has a solid stiff hoop, large enough for salmon, it will be so heavy as to overbalance in carrying. I came, therefore, to use a short-handled collapsible net: this was easy to carry, to detach and to make ready for use, when playing a fish. There are three serious drawbacks to this net. One is the shortness of the handle, a second is the comparatively restricted size and shallowness of the net. If the net itself is large and deep it will trail along the ground when it is collapsed and being carried, and thus get into many difficulties, including entanglement with the angler's feet. The third drawback is that in order to be collapsible, the net must be triangular in shape when expanded, and the end of it—the base of the triangle—be supported not by some hard rigid material, but some soft collapsible substance such as leather. With a net thus soft at the end the fish cannot be scooped out from above as it can be with a rigid hoop. These three drawbacks combined make it necessary for the angler to be so nearly or entirely on a level with the fish that he can place the net quite horizontally under it. Even so, the soft leather end yields when it touches the salmon, and has a tendency to tilt the body out of and not into the net. There befell me once a series of misfortunes with this net. I had hooked a good fish in a pool on the Cassley; there was no shelving bank on my side of the pool; the water was knee-deep right up to the bank, and the edge of the bank was a foot or more above the surface of the water. To get into position to net the fish, it was necessary to get into the water. I had wading stockings up to the thigh, which were sufficient. There was no slack water on this side of the pool. When the salmon showed signs of being exhausted I got into the water with the net ready below the fish, and with the help of the current easily drew it over the net.   But the leather end yielded, and at the critical moment I failed to get the fish into the net.   The salmon made a sudden recovery, and dashed down between my legs.   The first danger was to the rod.   To prevent this from snapping and to keep the line low and clear of my body, the point of the rod was at once lowered into the water, and to ease the strain on it I helped the line out with my hand.   The salmon was too tired to run far, but the position was absurd; the rod was pointing up stream—I was facing up stream—and some yards below me and behind me, where I could not see, was the salmon.   No one who has not been in this position can imagine how difficult it is for the angler to lift a wader-clogged leg over the line, to turn round, and to get himself once more into a dignified and appropriate position for playing the salmon that he still hopes will be his.   This being accomplished, I now held the fish in the stream, and reeled in line enough to enable me to get within reach of it.   But the process of netting a salmon in a fairly quick stream from above, and not from below, is difficult: in stretching down to get the net under the fish I fell flat in the water.   An angler's impulse when he falls is to use only one hand to save himself and to hold the rod up with the other.   The salmon was firmly hooked and very tired, and eventually I succeeded in getting it into the net and bringing everything to land, a wet but happy man, for the salmon was a good one for so small a river, and weighed 15 lb.   To an angler who had hooked a salmon for the first time, and had while playing it given it every conceivable chance of getting away, the experienced gillie, as at last he gaffed it, made the devastating comment: " He *would*na' go!" The same remark might have appropriately been made to me, but happily there was no one present to make it.

The pool on the Cassley that has been described above has the depressing name of the Cemetery Pool. Behind a few trees in a grass field on the left bank of the pool is a small enclosure; inside this is a burialground. There is no kirk or building of any sort near it, and but for the name of the pool an angler might fish for many a day without being aware of this little burialground, so secluded is it.

From the Cemetery Pool there is a short descent of rough water. There is nothing in this to obstruct the passage of salmon, but they do not like going up rough water until the temperature begins to rise in spring; and as a rule they do not go up this rough water until sometime in April; just as they do not, as a rule, face either of the great falls till May. The appearance of the first spring salmon in the Cemetery Pool often did not occur until the middle of April. This was always a great event, for till it happened one fished the Cemetery Pool with the depressing saying in mind: "It's ill work fishing when the fish'll no' take; and it's worse when they're no' there."

Below the rough water comes the Round Pool—a deep basin with rock bottom. The water enters in two streams, one slanting to the left and the other running close along the right bank. When the water is low the angler must fish each of these streams separately, and there is always a chance, even in very low water, that a fish may come in either of them.   In high water the two streams unite: there is slack water between them and the left bank, and the main outflow is a deep smooth glide to the left bottom corner.   From its smoothness, in contrast with the turbulent upper part of the stream, we called this "the glass"; and when the pool first became fishable after a spate in April, this spot was the greatest certainty (as far as anything in fishing can be certain) for getting a salmon that I have known on the Cassley or on any river.   Owing to the set of the current this spot, when in order, can be fished effectively only from the right bank, and at the head of the pool Providence has placed a large stone, large enough indeed to be dignified with the name of Rock.   It is smooth, very little above the level of the water, with ample room behind for over-head casting, and with a depression in the top of it which led to our calling it the "cup stone."   In this an angler can stand and thence command the whole pool, and finally, by raising the point of the rod, can hang the fly most attractively in "the glass."   There is still another expedient to be tried.   As a last resort the longest possible cast should be made to the bottom left-hand corner, and the line reeled up as slowly as the angler has patience to do it.   In any choice spot this method often succeeds when all else has failed.   When a fish has been hooked, the angler can step back on to the low bank, which is flush with the top of the cup stone, move down to the bottom of the pool, play the fish from this advantageous position, and finally draw it onto a bed of shingle which has been formed by a small burn that comes in immediately below the pool. If I were asked to name a place where Nature had, as if by design, done everything possible to please or help a salmon angler, I should say without doubt the Round Pool on the Cassley.

It would be a work of love, but tedious to a reader, to describe the other pools: three come below the Round Pool in quick succession; then there is a piece of fast water, shallow and unproductive, then the Bridge Pool, and then a pool called the Crag Pool, though on neither bank here is anything that can, by any reasonable use of the word, be called a crag. Seven pools in all, not counting the Falls Pool, that is of little account in April, and the whole contained in a distance of little, if at all, more than half a mile. All the pools are small as salmon pools go, but each differs from the rest in character, and needs to be fished in the method that experience has shown to be specially suited to it.

The best single day that we had on the Cassley was early in April 1919. The river had come into order after a big flood caused by melting snow. I had unfortunately to leave about four o'clock in the afternoon to go south. In the morning my brother had five fish, and I had four. After luncheon my brother got three more fish, and I got one before I left. After I had gone my brother got three more, making eleven salmon to his own rod.

The best days that I had personally were in the latter part of April 1911. Heavy showers kept the river up for nine continuous fishing days. In the first eight of them I got forty-four salmon. The best day gave me eight, and the worst four fish, and the day when I got four fish promised, at the outset, to be the best of all. I began fishing the Bridge Pool at 9.20, and by 10 o'clock I had three salmon on the bank, and felt, for the only time in my life about salmon fishing or any other experience in any sport, that if this went on all day it would be too much of a good thing. Then the river began to rise, and not till the rise of water ceased did I get another touch; and this was not till late in the evening, when I got one more fish.

On the ninth day a friend came to join me. He was to have come before, but had been detained in England, and I had promised him that on the day when he came I should leave the two best pools unfished till he arrived, and then see him catch a salmon in each of them. I passed and repassed the two pools as I went up and came down the right bank, and then passed and repassed them again as I went up and down the left bank in the morning, not without casting a longing eye on both each time, for they were in good order. One was the Round Pool, and the other a pool next but one below it, called—I know not why—the Big Lazy. From the other pools I got four fish.

My friend arrived shortly before two o'clock, and when he had lunched and put up his rod, we went straight to the Big Lazy. He rose and touched a fish half-way down the pool, but it came short; a few yards lower down he hooked and landed a salmon. In the Round Pool his fly reached "the glass" without touching anything, and then covered the place on which I relied to give him a fish. I feared the second half of my promise had failed. I urged my friend to cast again a little longer line, and a fish did come and was landed. It is seldom that anything in salmon fishing goes so entirely according to plan. On the next day the river had run down, but I got two fish, thus making fifty fish in ten consecutive fishing days, an average of five salmon a day, which is, no doubt, far from a record, but is good for spring fishing in this country.

And now, lest the picture should be too attractive to be truthful, let me confess that the Cassley has its defects. There is no loch to form a reservoir at its source, and unless it is constantly refreshed by rain or melting snow the river runs down very quickly. In April the Cemetery and Round Pools may give a fish occasionally, even in very low water, but in this condition in half an hour's fishing an angler will have exhausted all the possibilities. It can hardly be an exaggeration to say that in very low water a man in wading trousers, starting below the Round Pool, could walk down the middle of the river to the tidal pool at the mouth. So that an angler who visits the Cassley in a dry April may find that he gets not only hardly any fish, but hardly any fishing. For the trout fishing in that part of the river is worthless in April.

Owing to the small size of the pools there is not only no need, but in most of them no scope, for casting a long line. In the lower pools the bed of the river is too broad for a fly to be cast across the whole breadth, but even here the lie of the salmon can be easily covered from one bank or the other.

Unless, therefore, a salmon leaves the pool when being played, which it does only rarely, an angler never has, or

comes near to having, the excitement of seeing the
backing running off the reel.   Contrast this with the
sort of incident that happens in a big broad water, such
as the lower part of the Spey.   The angler is wading
and hooks a salmon, which bolts at speed straight across
the river.   Before it can have reached the opposite side
a lot of the backing is out: still it continues to run.
Presently a salmon shows itself — half plunge, half
jump.   It is incredible that this should be the angler's
fish, for it shows itself ten or twenty yards above the
place on the opposite side towards which the line is
pointing.   Nevertheless it is *the* fish, although the angler
has lost direct touch with it, and cannot tell by feel what
it is doing; can, indeed, feel nothing except the weight
of the drowned line and the pressure of the stream upon
it.   But this pressure tells upon the strength of the
salmon: it is heavy and unremitting, and yet the fish
cannot get a straight pull and break the line which is
curved in the stream.

That plunge on the surface was a sign that the
salmon could not make more headway: it still contests
every yard, but slowly and then more decidedly the
angler recovers line.   There is, however, little line left
on the reel.   The backing is very thin, and the amount
regained by each turn of the reel is very small: the main
line is buried far away out of sight, deep in the broad
stream: faster and faster does the angler reel as the fish
gives way more easily, and still the main line is invisible.
At such a time the thinness of the backing gives me a
sensation akin to terror.   The backing is in fact strong,
but it looks so frail!   Not till I feel the stouter main

line coming down through the rings and know that it is
winding on the reel do I feel comfortable. Even then
the salmon is some forty yards away, and may yet take
some backing out again, but if there are no dangerous
sunken rocks the odds are now heavily on the side of the
angler. He has by this time waded out onto the bank,
is able himself to move, and eventually to steer the fish
to a spot where it can easily be gaffed or netted. The
salmon which I have in mind in this description weighed
25 lb., and was caught in March, but such incidents are
more common later in the spring when the salmon are
more active than they are in the very cold weather and
water. There are no such supreme incidents on the
Cassley. On the Cassley in April there are very few
kelts indeed. On the Spey in March, or even in April,
there are very many. In seven fishing days early in
March 1929 I landed thirty-five kelts and only seven
clean fish. It is true that this was a very bad season;
nevertheless there are so many kelts in the Spey in March
that on hooking a fish my involuntary exclamation
is: "There's something!" On the Cassley it was:
"There he is!"

Below the Crag Pool there is yet half a mile of the
river before the Kyle is reached, and there are places
where salmon may be got now and then in a suitable
height of water, but all this lower part is of much less
interest. The good water in April is only half a mile,
with seven small pools. These can be fished three times
a day by one angler. When my brother was with me
they were therefore fished six times a day. No doubt
there is some monotony in this, but the drawback of so

limited an extent of water is not so great as might be supposed. When the pools are in order fresh fish may arrive from the Kyle at any hour of the day; and, however much the river has been fished in the morning and afternoon, two or three salmon may be found in the evening which have not seen a fly that day till then. This is especially true of the lower pools.

The Rosehall bank of the water on the beat of the Cassley described above has, I believe, passed into new ownership within the last year, and there have been other changes within recent years; changes there have been, too, on all the fishings I have known, but each has made a contribution to memory which is permanent.

CHAPTER XII

In the latter part of 1918 my last bit of centre vision was obscured and I descended at once on to a lower plane of sight than I had yet experienced. Since then there has been very slow deterioration, which is now perceptible even as compared with 1918; but the great drop came when the centre vision went: after that the difference between a little more and a little less side vision is one of degree. It does not add to the number of total disabilities that are imposed by the loss of centre vision. By 1918 I had ceased to be able to see a small fly floating on the water. It was, however, possible to judge distance more accurately and to present a dry fly effectively to a rising trout more frequently than I should have supposed to be possible under such disadvantage. Nevertheless, it happened more than once in this season that I struck to the sound of a rise without seeing it, and found that I had hooked the trout for which I was trying. It had taken my fly on the surface and I had failed to see the rise, even though my eyes had been directed to the place where I knew the fish to be. It was evident that for me the end of dry fly fishing was very near. It was so. When the season of 1919 came I could no longer see rises.

It would be possible still to get some trout on a dry fly with some one always in attendance to help me. The attendant would find a rising trout, would show me where to stand or to kneel: would describe the direction in and the distance to which the fly should be cast: would say when this had been done correctly: and finally would utter some exclamation when the fish took the fly, so that I might give the necessary strike. But the whole process would be intolerably cumbersome and clumsy, and I should bungle sadly. Skill in dry fly fishing is denied to bad sight.

Nec vera virtus, cum semel exidit,
curat reponi deterioribus.

There remains wet fly fishing for trout in still water and across or down stream. When there is no slack line, a certain proportion of trout—a good proportion when they are taking well—that come at an angler's fly will hook themselves. There is, of course, some bungling. With indistinct vision it is not easy to place the landing net accurately under a trout, even when the fish is exhausted and can be held steady on the surface of the water, especially if this be a rippling stream. More than once recently, when wading in such water, where trout average four to the pound, has the mistake been made of placing the net carefully under a bit of foam, which, as the net was lifted, dissolved and disappeared like a mocking spirit. Nevertheless, the thing can be done still, independent and unaided, which is an essential part of the peculiar pleasure of trout fishing: and though my baskets are light there come bright gleams of success. The mere touch of a trout, even if it does not hook itself, gives a little thrill; the feel of a small, single-handed rod, its quick and delicate motion, and its response to the hand, are delightful: it is very pleasant to spend a day by rippling streams with a background of trees and the air lively with the songs of birds in April and May.

Salmon fishing is less difficult, though some of the pleasure is gone. It is twelve years since I have been able to see my fly fall on the water or to watch the line. These things were a matter of course in salmon fishing: not till I lost sight of them did I realize what an integral part of the interest of salmon fishing they were. The salmon angler watches the fall of his fly at each cast, and his eyes are ever on the draw of the stream on his line. To be deprived of the latter is an even greater loss than it is to be unable to see the fly fall on the water.

However good be the river or the beat on it, there must be many hours, and an occasional day, when the angler does not get a pull: and to fish hour after hour seeing only the rod and nothing of the line is a very blank business. On days of failure an angler may be said to go through four stages of feeling. He begins with Expectation: this is presently modified to Hope: after Hope has been long deferred the angler subsides into the stage of Resignation: finally as the day draws to a close he sinks into Despair. The angler who fishes without seeing his fly or line passes more quickly through the happier to the lower stages.

Every angler loses a certain proportion of the salmon that he hooks and plays. There are days of hard luck

and of good luck in this matter, but taking figures
over a period of days I used to estimate that my proportion of fish lost to fish landed was one in six. For
example, in the ten good days on the Cassley, described
in the preceding chapter, sixty salmon were hooked and
fifty landed. Two of the ten salmon that escaped broke
the line round rocks. As the hook had sufficiently firm
hold to break a strong gut cast, it may be assumed
that but for the exceptional misfortune of the rocks,
these two fish would have been landed. Eight in sixty
would thus have been the proportion of salmon lost
owing to the hook coming out. This is not a proportion that should cause excessive annoyance, and I
do not remember having suffered greatly from losing
salmon before my sight was impaired. Since that time
I have suffered very badly. In one black week on the
Cassley a few years ago, out of twenty-two salmon
hooked only seven were landed. None of those that
escaped broke the line: the fly just came away un-
accountably, often when the fish was almost within
reach of the net.

In speaking of salmon "hooked" I include only the
fish that have been actually played. Those that come
to the surface immediately after being struck and splash
themselves free are not counted; nor indeed are any
salmon counted as "lost" if they have been held for
quite a short time. In other words, only fish that have
been not only hooked but played have been included in
the calculation of fish lost. My experience that week
was such as I hope no other angler may have to endure.
A week that might have been happy and successful was

turned to misery. My brother, who was fishing with me, hooked at least as many fish in those same six days, but did not lose an undue proportion and had a good week.

Things are, of course, not always so bad as in that week, or I should not be salmon fishing still. Nevertheless, the number of salmon hooked and played that I lose has been for the last twelve years very harassing. I cannot imagine why impaired sight should have caused this. It is not by sight, but by feel, that an angler strikes a salmon. In spring, salmon as a rule take the fly under water unseen: even if a fish does make a visible rise, the angler should not strike till the pull is felt. For this purpose it is an advantage not to see the rise. Why, then, should bad sight cause me to fail to hook fish securely? I can only suggest that the angler who watches the line coming round in the stream sees unconsciously, or half-consciously, the line tighten at the instant when he feels the pull of a fish: and that eyes and hands both being alert he strikes with more conviction than if he only felt and did not see. And to strike with conviction and not tentatively is necessary to hook salmon securely, especially with the big hooks that are used in spring.

Certainly since my sight was impaired I neither hook nor land as many fish as I used to do in comparison with others. The adverse change in this respect was very noticeable and persistent when my brother fished with me on the Cassley, where we could compare present with past experience on the same water. Some success I still have, but the conclusion is irresistible that when a man ceases to be able to see what he is doing he does not do so well as he did before. The new method of salmon fishing with a greased line and comparatively small rod and fly presumably requires better sight than the ordinary method, and I have not tried it. It is by repute, and I dare say in practice, very effective, particularly in low water.

As long as there is a fair chance of getting fish the pleasure of fly fishing is to a very keen angler inexhaustible. It was, I think, Dr. Johnson who complained that he had never in his life had enough peaches. He therefore never knew, and we can never know, how many peaches would have satisfied him. In like manner, I shall never know for how many days I could fish continuously without wearying of it. Trout fishing has always been intermittent: of spring salmon fishing I have had, as a rule, from ten to twenty days in the season, and not more than ten days at a time. Would a keen golfer be satisfied if he played golf on from ten to twenty days only in the year? I suspect he would not, and I am sure that this allowance of salmon fishing is not satisfying. On the occasions when I have had a continuous spell of salmon fishing, I have quitted the river with as much regret at the end of the fifth or sixth week as I should have felt at the end of the first.

On the other hand, one does become more fastidious as to the kind of sport. To catch fresh run salmon spoils the interest in red or dark fish. The latter may give good sport, but to land a tarnished fish when an angler has been used to the brilliant excellence of fresh run spring salmon, gives a sense of dissatisfaction that blunts the edge of keenness.

Most men have to earn their own living and have little enough opportunity for indulging in pleasure, even if they have keenness. But any really keen angler who has not had to work from necessity, and yet has not spent the whole of each season in fly fishing, may say, as Clive said when he reflected on his opportunities of acquiring wealth in India, that he is astonished at his own moderation.

The moderation imposed on any one who undertakes important work in life may be very distressing. I recall, in particular, a certain bitter moment in the latter half of April 1909. In 1906 and 1907 I had had no spring salmon fishing at all. In 1908 I had ten days, but the Cassley was low: I got only two salmon: in the whole time there was hardly any water in which to throw a fly. My days were spent walking about the moors in the April sunshine. "Not a bad way of spending a holiday," some one may say. True, but it was not the thing for which I had paid rent or which I had come to do, and it was not satisfying to a man who had not caught a spring salmon for three years.

In 1909 I came to the Cassley again and this time the river was in order. After three years of abstinence or failure the prospect of good fishing was before me. On the first day I had five fish by four o'clock; this was equal to the best day I had ever had up to that time. The little post office where I was staying was only a hundred yards from the river. I came in to see what the Foreign Office had sent me.

There was an alarmist telegram about the state of things in Constantinople. I decided that I must return to London. It was then too late to get the evening train: I went back to the river and got one more salmon, making what was then a record for me. The next morning I left: the river was still in order; there was the prospect of a week of good sport if only I could stay: there was the certainty that I must wait a whole year before I could spring-salmon fish again. And there was not even the compensation of feeling a martyr to duty. If the disturbances at Constantinople became dangerous, British action must be limited to protecting British lives and property. The measures necessary for this would be taken by the diplomatic and naval authorities on the spot, whether I were at the Foreign Office or not. If I stayed at the Cassley till something really happened I could be at the Foreign Office in plenty of time to deal with political complications that might arise later on, the public interest would not suffer if I awaited developments. But the fear of what would be said in the House of Commons and in the Press, if something did happen and I were absent from my office, destroyed my equanimity: I went back to London feeling cowardly rather than noble, and not at all convinced that the sacrifice made was necessary. The event proved that it was unnecessary.

Such misfortune and disappointment leaves a mark on memory, but it is an isolated incident. When the angler looks back he sees a long vista of happy days: by a special act of memory he can select individual days of outstanding success, but even these seem not to be exceptions; they are but contributory parts of an enjoyment that was greater than any single day could contain. For to an angler as he looks back his angling days seem to belong to a world different from, and fairer, than the world in which he has worked. In retrospect the surroundings, the country, the beauty of river scenes are an inseparable part of the pleasure. The keen angler may indeed be comparatively indifferent to them when actively engaged in fishing. If a rare and beautiful bird had appeared in a Hampshire water meadow when trout were rising and I was busy with them, what would the effect on my fishing have been? My impression is that I should have made a mental note of it, resolved to look for and watch the bird when the rise of trout was over, and have continued to fish without interruption. So intense is the interest and excitement of fly fishing when we are actively engaged in it. On the other hand, if I could again fish with a dry fly I should not now take a fishing, unless it was in beautiful country. The fact that the water meadows where I fished on the Itchen were one of the fairest spots in the world became an ever-increasing part in the enjoyment. This enhanced the anticipation of going thither; it made the days spent there radiant.

The cottage that I put up by the Itchen in 1890 was intended only as a fishing cottage; a place in which to get food, sleep, and shelter when I was not fishing. It became a sanctuary. The peace and beauty of the spot made it a sacred place. The cottage belongs to angling memories, but the fishing became a small part of the happiness that was associated with it. For thirty-three years the chosen spot remained a place of refuge and delight, not in the fishing season only. For the last four years, indeed, I had been unable to fish with a dry fly, and the original purpose for which the cottage had been put there had ceased to be. Great changes, however, had been taking place that were inseparable from a new epoch. For the first fifteen years there was little change and had been little change for many years before this time. I had seen the old mill at the village not far away replaced by a new building, and the dull, monotonous sound of a turbine had replaced the lively splashing of a water-wheel; but otherwise things remained as they were. The cottage was invisible from any road; it was approached by an old lime avenue, long disused, and the track down this was not suited for any wheels but those of a farm cart. There was a little wayside station on a single railway line close by; but the quickest route from London was to go by a fast train to Winchester, and thence to drive a distance between four and five miles to the nearest point to the cottage that was accessible by wheels. This was a drive of at least half an hour in a one-horse fly. Presently taxi-cabs took the place of the horse conveyance and reduced the time of the drive to a quarter of an hour. Was this an advantage? On balance it was not. For escape from London meant that hurry, noise and bustle had been left behind: I had entered into leisure, where saving of time was no object, and often I would walk from Winchester to enjoy the country. There was a footpath way on each side of the river. By one of these one entered the cottage without, except for the momentary crossing of one road and of three secluded lanes, having had touch or sight of a road. There were thirty-three stiles on this path. It happened not infrequently that I could not get to Winchester till the latest train arriving there some time after eleven o'clock. The walk then lasted well into the midnight hour. In the dusk or dark it was easier to walk by the road than by the path. There was much charm in this midnight walk. Traffic had ceased, cottage lights had been put out, the inmates were all at rest or asleep. Now and then one heard in passing the song of a nightingale or a sedge-warbler, but in the main there was silence. It was pleasant after the hardness of London streets and pavements to feel the soft dust about my feet. On a still summer night there were sweet and delicate scents in the air, breathed forth from leaves and herbs and grass, and from the earth itself. It was as if one's own very being was soothed and in some way refined by the stillness, the gentleness and the sweetness of it all.

Then came the age of motors and tarred roads. Few people, I imagine, seek the smell of tar for its own sake. To me there is nothing unclean or nauseous in it, but it is a coarse, rough smell. The sweet and delicate scents of the night were obliterated by it, as if, overpowered and repelled, they had sunk back into the leaves and earth from which they had ventured into air. The strong smell of the tar seemed to disturb even the stillness of the night: the soft dust was no more, and the road was hard as a paved street. Not all, but much of the charm of the night walk was gone. There were other changes too; small houses of the villa type were built along the road that was nearest to the cottage: doubtless there are more of them now, for the cottage was accidentally destroyed by fire in January 1923, and I have not seen the place for some years. The sense of change was in the air. It may be that change is for the good:

> The old order changeth, yielding place to new,
> And God fulfils himself in many ways,
> Lest one good custom should corrupt the world.

It is not for us, who cannot foresee the future, who perhaps cannot rightly understand the present, to chide or to repine too much. Only it is impossible for us, who in our youth gave our affections to things that are passed or passing away, to transfer our affections to new things in which a new generation finds delight.

The beauty, however, of chalk-stream valleys still remains wonderful. The river still waters meadows that are unspoilt and unchanged, and its clear purity is guarded and protected.

> Still glides the stream and shall for ever glide,
> The form remains, the function never dies.

Thus, as the angler looks back he thinks less of individual captures and days than of the scenes in which he fished. The luxuriance of water meadows, animated by insect and bird and trout life, tender with the green and gay with the blossoms of early spring: the nobleness and volume of great salmon rivers: the exhilaration of looking at any salmon pool, great or small; the rich brownness of Highland water: the wild openness of the treeless, trackless spaces which he has traversed in an explorer's spirit of adventure to search likely water for sea trout: now on one, now on another of these scenes an angler's mind will dwell, as he thinks of fishing. Special days and successes he will no doubt recall, but always with the remembrance and the mind's vision of the scenes and the world in which he fished. For, indeed, this does seem a separate world, a world of beauty and enjoyment. The time must come to all of us, who live long, when memory is more than prospect. An angler who has reached this stage and reviews the pleasure of life will be grateful and glad that he has been an angler, for he will look back upon days radiant with happiness, peaks and peaks of enjoyment that are not less bright because they are lit in memory by the light of a setting sun.

INDEX